MW01101214

Stories of
Transformation
and
Hope

Stories of
Transformation
and
Hope

Mary's Gospel

Irene Alexander

WIPF & STOCK · Eugene, Oregon

STORIES OF TRANSFORMATION AND HOPE
Mary's Gospel

Copyright © 2013 Irene Alexander. All rights reserved. Except for brief
quotations in critical publications or reviews, no part of this book may
be reproduced in any manner without prior written permission from the
publisher. Write: Permissions, Wipf and Stock Publishers, 199 W. 8th Ave.,
Suite 3, Eugene, OR 97401.

Wipf & Stock
An Imprint of Wipf and Stock Publishers
199 W. 8th Ave., Suite 3
Eugene, OR 97401

www.wipfandstock.com

ISBN 13: 978-1-62564-544-9

Manufactured in the U.S.A.

All scripture quotations unless otherwise noted are from the NRSV Bible.

Contents

Acknowledgments

IN THESE STORIES I have taken the actual words in the gospels and kept them. The stories are set in Jesus' time. But I have imagined the background to each person, and filled this out so they become a real person, bringing the stories to life, and the people into our present reality, and most of all bringing Jesus into real encounters with real people like us.

Many people have listened to, read and commented on these stories, and I thank them for their comments, suggestions, and especially their tears.

Most of all I would like to thank our writers' retreat, Charles Ringma, Jill Manton, Chris Brown, and Terry Gatfield—they have encouraged me, disagreed with me, and corrected me. I am very grateful for their input—even though I have chosen my own stories and details in the end. Thank you to Kennedy Warne for his support and titles and helping me over a hurdle on the journey.

I am grateful to Christian Amondson at Wipf and Stock who is continuing to publish books in the face of much adversity in the publishing world.

A special thanks to Carrie Sinclair Wolcott for her thoughtful and thorough editing, and to Karen Hollenbeck Wuest for her early guidance and suggestions.

1

Mary's Introduction

THERE HAVE ALREADY BEEN written and circulated many stories of the life and death and living again of the Son of God, Jesus of Nazareth. He led us into a new way of seeing life, understanding the kingdom of God, and relating to a God of love beyond our imagining. But these stories have been passed from mouth to mouth, from town to town, from community to community. And some stories have diminished in the telling, while others have been exaggerated or distorted.

So I, who knew many of the people of whom the tales were told, have decided to tell of Jesus' life and Jesus' way, by gathering stories—stories of people's remembering, directly from them. These are the stories of those who lived it, those who saw with their own eyes and touched with their own hands, those whose lives were changed by his life lived in their very presence.

So here they are: Elisabeth and Andrew, Nicodemus, Zacchaeus, and Thomas—and the ones whose names you've never heard. You may have heard of them, but only as the woman at the well, the woman who washed Jesus' feet with her tears, the widow of Nain, the man born blind, the Syrophoenician woman.

All these nameless ones I had met, and I sought out as many as I could so you could hear their stories—hear them from the inside. That your own story—the one you know from the inside—may be gilded with his touch, with the Love poured out. You, too, can be touched by a God who stoops to lift us and turn our faces up to see the face of the loving Creator and the love in those eyes. Know it as love for you.

Let me start by telling you a little of myself, Mary, from Magdala in Galilee. There have been all sorts of rumors about me—that being from Magdala, a Roman garrison town, meant that I must be a prostitute. That having seven evil spirits cast out of me proved I must have been caught in sexual sin. I don't remember ever hearing that the man with the legion of demons cast out must have been in sexual sin. But that is the way of the world in our time—to sexualize women or to minimize them, to take away their voices. It was not the way of Jesus of Nazareth.

I was indeed very low when I met him, weakened by years of battling with chronic illness, the ensuing anxiety and fear, and the tendency to be laid low with any disease that others carried. My friend Susanna asked Jesus to come to my home with her. He came and listened to my story. Then, laying his hand on my head and praying to God the father of us all, he healed me. As I opened my eyes and looked into his I found myself in a place of deeper peace than I had ever known. I looked outside and it was as though the world was washed in brighter colors, the weight I had carried in my body for years had been lifted and I felt light and clean. I remember laughing, laughing with the sparkling joy of a new life. I remember he laughed too, and Susanna joined in. From that first moment it was as though he and I shared the deepest secret, a secret of profound joy. We could return to it again simply by meeting each other's eyes.

When he left after that initial meeting, Susanna told me more of him. How he was traveling with a group of disciples around the towns and villages of Galilee and Judea, healing people, and teaching about the kingdom. I had had nothing much of a life for years, and in my new self-assurance and energy I impulsively announced, "Susanna, I want to go with them." "But we can't," she said, "they're traveling all the time, and, and . . ." She was obviously trying to think of reasons. "What will people say?" "Susanna, people say all sorts of things about me already. Oh, Susanna! I so want to hear more about the kingdom. And, I'll admit it, I want to be around this man."

Susanna could not think of reasons not to go and we had the means to do it; in the end, there came to be many women who traveled on and off at different times. Oh, I know you don't hear of us mentioned in many of the stories, but we were there traveling with the men. Sometimes we were welcomed and sometimes not, but we were always included by Jesus.[1] For that period he became my life. I cannot describe what it was like to go from those blank years when life was stretched so thin, to such a spiritual, physical, emotional, and intellectual richness. As we walked he would tell stories that pointed to the kingdom, to the way life could be if we all lived with God as sovereign in our lives. If we would live in relation to God as beloved father-mother—both individually and also together—we would be living the kingdom. I was utterly captivated, both by the *idea* of actually living like that, and by him. The concepts by themselves would have been intriguing to me, but his embodiment of them changed it from theory to actual, enthralling, confronting reality. The sense I had had on coming to healing, coming to faith, was that I had discovered a profound secret. It was as though I glimpsed the truth of all this in his very being, in his utter knowing of this God and the truth of the kingdom. And what fascinated me was that it connected with a deep knowing of my own. I discovered some inchoate wisdom that this *is* what God is like and this *is* how life can be lived, if it is to be lived in all its fullness.

Of course, living life in this fullness is different for each person. If I was to help others find the fullness of this kingdom life, I needed to have some understanding of the different journeys people traveled: the varied encounters they had with Jesus, the ways they responded to his life-giving touch and his transforming vision

1. Luke 8:2–3.

of the kingdom, and the invitations they received into intimacy with our Father God. I wanted others to be able to glimpse the exquisite transformation that takes place when a person interacts with this living God and journeys with the living Jesus. What happens when he enters the reality of each individual life and teaches us to share his yoke and walk in his way?

The incident that started me on this gathering of others' stories was my interaction with Nicodemus. When I first heard of Nicodemus, I was afraid that he might be secretly finding ways to ensnare Jesus as other Pharisees did in the public confrontations. But as time went on, we heard of his support and I began to wonder what he was really like. I only saw him briefly, a few times. One of the men pointed him out to me once in the temple; later, I saw him when there was a crowd of us in Bethany. I didn't actually meet him until that awful evening as we prepared Jesus' body for burial. Deep in my own grief and horror, I had little room in my heart for him. Nevertheless, something of his own deep devotion to Jesus seeped into my consciousness even then.

It was only later, after Jesus' risen life had washed through every cell of my being, that I began to try to piece together the story of the transformation that had taken place in Nicodemus. With the joy of resurrection life alive in me, and in curiosity about how his slow conversion had come about, I asked him to tell me the whole story.[2] It was that recounting that wakened to me the possibility of hearing and sharing the hidden stories, the narratives of men and women I had met along the way as I had traveled with Jesus.

---

2. I have told my version of Nicodemus' story in Alexander, Irene, *A Glimpse of the Kingdom in Academia: Academic Formation as Radical Discipleship*. Eugene, OR: Cascade, 2013.

2

An Ordinary Woman,
an Extraordinary Drama

Elisabeth[1]

As THIS IDEA OF gathering others' stories began to grow within me, my thoughts turned to Elisabeth, the mother of John the Baptizer. Mary, Jesus' mother, had told me of her. It was to Elisabeth that she herself had turned when she had first dared to believe she was pregnant with the Holy One. Apart from Mary, Elisabeth was the first to know of the coming of the Messiah. Her immediate recognition of the presence of the holy in Mary's womb made me want to test out the idea that was growing within me. I decided to seek her out and, if she was still alive, lay before her, and the Holy Spirit within her, this possibility of gathering stories that would help others know the Messiah. And if she would tell me her story—why, that could be the beginning of my narrative!

Over the years since that beginning, I sought out other followers who, like me, had been transformed by the touch of the God-become-man, had traveled with him, and had encountered

---

1. From Luke 1, 3, Matthew 14:1–12.

him in those short years of his life among us. I have retold them here, writing them down as close to their telling as I am able to recall. I want you to experience the embodying of the love relationship Jesus had with our God, and I hope you will sense how the kingdom can be lived in the everyday life of ordinary people.

But I get ahead of myself. Back in those early years after the resurrection, as I listened to people's stories and told and retold the words of Jesus, I stayed mostly in Jerusalem with the other believers. Bands of us would sometimes travel to visit and encourage groups of new believers or others who asked us to tell of the way of Jesus. As I settled on this idea of gathering stories and seeking out those whose lives had been transformed, I looked for an opportunity to visit Elisabeth.

When at last I made my way up the winding road to her village in the Judean hills—a road I knew Mary must have taken those decades earlier—I had a sense of possibility and excitement, but trepidation too. I feared that she might have died or that she might think my idea impossible or unnecessary. But the moment I greeted her and met those shining dark eyes buried in folds of wrinkled skin, I knew she would understand what was being birthed within me. She bid me stay with her. The next day, after a deep sleep, she led me to a quiet corner where the sun warmed the wall at our backs, and she began her story.

Elisabeth's Story

Tell me your story, you say. Tell me the story of a very old woman looking back down the years. What changes I have seen. What a different world I look back on over the years, different yet the same—marriages and births, sickness and death, joy and sorrow. These are the same, with different faces, different details. Sometimes I see a girl in the street and I think I recognize her, only to remember she is long since dead, or old, or a mother herself. My life, so different from what I expected, is a variation on the same themes: love and marriage, birth and death, grief and unexpected joy.

Where shall I begin? I grew up here, not too far from Jerusalem, with the rhythm of the feasts patterning our days. My parents, of the tribe of Aaron, were observant and brought us up to follow the laws and to attend all we could of the feast days in Jerusalem. When it came my time to marry, they were very happy to find a young man of the priestly line. And I too was content. I loved the festivals and songs and scriptures that wove our people together. I can't say I liked all the slaughtering of cattle around the feasts, but I understood that there is no forgiveness of sins without the shedding of blood. The stories of our people's captivity and freedom, exile and return, have always been the tapestry into which my life is woven.

I picture it that way—a vast tapestry of the stories of our people from our first parents, to the captivity in Egypt, to the giving of the law and the feast days that form such a framework for our lives and for the generations. And I see my life as one little thread woven in and out of dark images and into the golden light, even while entwined in shadow. And if you can stand back as I do now, you will see the whole—pictures of oppression and pain, of darkness and light, of sin and generosity—all woven into the story of ordinary men and women, yet linked somehow with a God who stoops into the ordinary.

That is the story of my life—of an ordinary woman playing a small part in an extraordinary drama played out in our towns and villages, our streets and our hearts. It is a story that changes all of history, the whole story of humankind. I am in awe that I have been on stage at such a time as this, seeing history turn on the hinge of our generation to let the light of Almighty God flood in.

But let me start at the beginning. I married, as I said, into a priestly line—Zechariah, of Abijah's line. As is the custom, I went to live with his family and learn from them what it meant to be the wife of a priest. It meant living together among the everyday, extended family and then losing him for a time as he went and served in the temple. When he was gone, I was simply to be another member of the family—helping with the meals and the children, the sick and the old, serving in whatever way came to me. I remember it was lonely at first. I was a new sister and daughter in a family I hardly knew, among others who each knew their place. But I watched and learned and contributed.

I remember vividly those first couple of years: others became pregnant and had children, mothered their children and became more themselves, and found their place in the fabric of our extended family. I helped look after their children and stepped in when someone was sick—each month I hoped it was my turn. Those first years I was expectant. I believed I, too, would soon be pregnant and, with my children, would be part of the interweaving of family and generation. I tried not to show any of the anxiety I felt, but sometimes one of the old grandmothers would read my face and say, "Your time will come my dear." Her words, intending comfort, would bring quick tears, even while I was grateful for her kindness.

As those first years went by, it became more evident that I would not have children. My husband said little, but he asked me now and then, with the awkward bluntness some men have. I knew he tried not to blame me, but I felt it anyway. He saw it as a shortcoming on my part and I heard it in his voice if the subject of children came up with someone who did not know us.

I carried the pain of it deep within me. I prayed to the God of Sarah and Rachel—they knew childlessness. I prayed Hannah's prayer, and begged the God of fruitfulness to give me children. I promised my child to him. I prayed the many names of God and listened to the scriptures for any hint I was missing. I asked for the wind of the Spirit to bring life to my womb and for the mothering El Shaddai to make me a mother. I entreated the God of Isaiah to give me a child whom I could hold close as my very own. All the while, I joined the everyday life around me with all possible cheerfulness, trying not to show the painful longing hidden within.

Maybe it was those years of hiding pain and trying to stay open to the Spirit of God that helped me see the pain in others; perhaps I would have been like that anyway. Others began to come to me with their anxieties and hurts. I tried to make a gentle place of listening, of openness to the generous Spirit of God, of welcome for whatever hurt or weakness or sin. I remember noticing how often the scriptures told of such a God as this—if only we had the ears to hear.

When I look back I see what a sheltered time that was. Of course the Romans occupied our country, but in the hills where I have lived all these years with my extended family, we had little dealings with them. When we went down to Jerusalem for the feast days, it was a different story, but I kept myself well away from them. I think Zechariah protected me from the worst of the stories.

Gradually, I gave up hope of being a mother. Well, not totally—every now and then I would find myself wishing, hardly daring to hope. But I was always disappointed. I learned to bring this to God and to welcome another invitation to trust God's grace in the midst of not understanding. It became something of a secret sacrament between God and me. Each month I learned to speak my trust in a God who does not give what I long for. The words of Habakkuk became my inner heart song, "Though the fig tree does not blossom, and there be no herd in the stall, yet will I rejoice in the Lord."[2]

Sometimes my rejoicing was threaded with tears, but I came to deeply know the God who was trustworthy even in the darkness; the hidden places of my pain became a place of intimacy and gratitude. So I found I could be with others and not be afraid of their pain, of their loss. I could be with those facing death, listen to their stories, and trust that, somehow, the God who is Life held all.

And then came my own miracle of life. There was no angelic visitation for me, and I only found out later what had happened to Zechariah. At the time, all I knew was that he came back from the temple, and as it were, turned inward into himself, and not speaking to anyone at all. There was an intentness in his lovemaking that had only been there in the early years, and I guessed that something had happened between him and God. I had already begun to bleed less often with age; other signs in my body began to make me wonder. I kept my hopes to myself and told no one except God, the mothering God who knew my longings and fears before I voiced them.

2. From Habakkuk 3:17–18.

Even when I began to be sure it was pregnancy, I feared it was some sickness or tumor growing within. Such things had happened to others, and the part of me that still carried the shame at my barrenness was afraid. So I kept to myself those five months, holding it between God and me. I told Zechariah only when I thought it must be so. But I told no one else—until, suddenly, Mary appeared with a secret of her own.

Let me tell you of Mary. She was the child of a cousin of mine. I saw her over the years when her family came to Jerusalem for the feasts. I watched her grow up like others of the family. She obviously had a heart for God—I saw the intensity of her listening and the reality of her faith as she sang the psalms. I remember her asking me some question about the will of God—I saw the openness of her heart as she tried to understand. I remember thinking that she too was one who held questions gently in her heart, waiting in faith for answers that may or may not come.

I heard of her betrothal to Joseph and was grateful she was promised to one who also honored God and sought his ways. Though I did not expect to see her until after her marriage and after my child's birth, one day she appeared. I will never forget the look on that young face. It was a questioning look, shy and radiantly joyful at once, that showed she knew more than one would expect in one so young. She was hardly more than a child, and yet she had a look of inward knowing, even as she questioned. As I turned toward her standing in the doorway, my own heart leaped as the child within me leaped for joy. I cannot tell you how I knew this, but I did. "Oh, Mary! You carry our God within you," I said, and both of us burst into the kind of laughter that cannot be kept inside. There in my ordinary, everyday life of bread and vegetables and cooking, I took in my arms the wonder of all of history—a God who comes to the womb of a girl. This was a God who becomes one of us, opens our eyes, and reveals the sacred everywhere.

Sitting Mary down, I asked her to tell me her story. Instead, she answered with a question of her own. "Oh, Elisabeth, is it true that you are going to have a child?" No one knew except Zechariah, and I knew he would have told no one. I did not answer her directly. I remember sitting very still and saying, "Tell me why you ask?" Out tumbled her story—joy and tears, questions and words from the psalms, and finally, "Elisabeth, if you're pregnant too, then I know it is all true, and I'm not making all this up."

So there it was. Her question was the answer to my question, and my answer the answer to hers. "Yes, Mary. I am pregnant, and my child leaped within me when you came to the door just now." Tears ran down my face as I finally spoke the truth of my own pregnancy. "Oh, Mary! What faith you have, to believe God in this." I asked her to stay with me those months. When I finally began to tell others that I was indeed pregnant, I noticed them wondering whether this child may have a special purpose from God.

Mary stayed with me and we sifted the scriptures together to make sense of the promise she had been given. By then there was no doubting that she was pregnant and we spoke of how she would tell her family and her fiancé of this. Courageous young woman she was, I saw the firmness as she lifted her chin and spoke her faith in a God who would care for her. She refused to receive the shame that others would turn on her and determinedly spoke of the blessing of God and her expectation of his protection and promises.

It was a precious and intimate time. Ours was an unlikely friendship with thirty years between us. We shared the most special months of our lives and celebrated the holy carried within each of us. Together we learned of God as the One who is present. We would talk as ordinary life went on around us. We talked of the God of light and of darkness, of joy and of suffering, a God of both mystery and pure abundant love. Sometimes I feared for her, knowing her life must be complicated by misunderstanding and judgment, but she would look at me with a kind of knowing innocence and say, "But God is with us; isn't that everything?"

Over the months she stayed, we shared deeply. She would tell me of her ponderings, and I would tell her mine. In the end, I shared with her more than I had with anyone—I let her see the shame I had carried and the inner trust it had formed in me. She helped me in those last months when I began to feel clumsy and tired, and her excitement at her own pregnancy allowed me to share my own. We knew that the child we each carried within was a gift of God, and we knew too that there was a special purpose for our children that we could only guess. We believed that somehow the purposes were intertwined. I wondered if my own waiting had been a waiting for the fullness of time—for her to be ready. I didn't understand what any of that meant at the time, but Mary's ever-present sense of gladness gave my quieter faith an expectation that God would bring goodness for both of us.

When the time came for my son to be born, Mary headed home. In all these months Zechariah had been preoccupied with his own dealings with God, but when our son was born he named him John. "God is gracious," he said, standing up to others who wanted one of the traditional names of the family. I knew he had found a place of trust and responsiveness.

Those first few years I was totally immersed in being a mother. I was older and I tired easily. I knew, like Hannah, that my son was only loaned to me for a short time and I wanted to savor every moment. He was an unusual child, even from a very young age. Serious and intent, he asked the most unusual questions. I sensed that his life was for a specific purpose and this kept me attentive to him. Zechariah and I would try to explain all we could in response to his many questions about nature, people, the temple, the law, God, the scriptures, and the stories of our people. He learned the scriptures easily, but was not content with just reciting them. He wanted to know the meaning of everything.

Zechariah had said from the beginning that he was to be consecrated to God, like the Nazarites of old. Hannah's story had prepared me for that—I knew this child, given to me by God, would always be His. I tried to hold him with open hands. I saw him as coming from God and going to God, but still I prayed for a long and happy life for him. Yet, even as I prayed, I suspected it would not be so. I knew for Mary's son it could not be so—it was easier to sense this for someone else than for myself.

When we met, our sons would play together: my John, intent and more solitary, and her Jesus, lighter somehow, yet with a depth unusual in a child. I would watch and wonder, and together we would pray that the gracious God would work in and through their lives. They would sit with Zechariah, questioning him about the law and about the temple. One or the other of them would want to know if the way people lived was really how God had said they should. I would listen in the background and hear Zechariah challenged by things he had taken for granted. It was harder for him to bend, steeped as he was in the traditional ways and getting old by then. He tried to listen and respond as best he could.

Zechariah told me, with some pride, of Jesus coming to the temple the year the boys were twelve. We had all gone to the feast of the Passover, that year. Our families intermingled and swapped stories of the previous year. When John and Zechariah returned home—I had returned earlier, with the mothers and younger children—they told me how Jesus had stayed behind and gone daily to the temple to question the priests and religious leaders. I could imagine it, the way he and John questioned Zechariah: following the thread of an argument, refusing easy answers, always going below the surface of custom, and wanting to know God's deeper purposes and meanings. I imagined him asking the Passover questions about Elijah the prophet and the coming of the Messiah. The prophets had wanted to know how they would know of his coming. I could imagine the priests, at once irritated and intrigued by this boy's questioning.

Zechariah began to believe he would die before John reached adulthood. He asked me to promise that John would receive the training he needed. Zechariah believed the Nazarites living in the desert could prepare John for the life he was called into. I was not as convinced as he was, but I trusted his desire to please the God who had so clearly spoken to him before John's conception.

After Zechariah's death, soon after John's coming of age, I lost them both. I had to gather the threads of my life into another pattern. Motherhood changed my position in our community. Becoming a widow changed it again. I found my place again in the interweavings of the families. I became an extra grandmother to the little children, a listening ear for the young women. I watched for the ones others did not see or the ones who did not fit.

At first, I saw John every year when we went to Jerusalem. I could see how his thoughts were forming as he argued and debated with the men. At times, I thought he would join the Essenes or the Zealots—his ideas were so strong and outspoken. In the end, he joined no sect. He saw the weaknesses in all of them and demanded a way of living that most people could not reach. He lived it, though, a self-discipline that was almost harsh. For a time there was a hardness in him, a criticism that our people did not live as God had commanded us. He would state angrily that we deserved the oppression we were under because of our refusal to live righteous lives. Over time the hardness lessened.

He was living mostly in the wilderness beyond the Jordan and learning of the God of Abraham, Isaac, and Jacob. That's what he would speak about when we had time together. By then, I found the journey to Jerusalem too arduous. To see me, he had to travel the road up into the hills. He had come to respect the wisdom I had learned along my journey—not that I could enter an argument like he did. He came to see that I knew our God—the God of our ancestors who meets us in the real pains and challenges of our lives. And he began to question what I understood of death and injustice and loss. I told him of the gracious God of mystery and presence, even in the darkness. He was less interested in the questions that didn't have answers. He saw that we could do so much if only we would: share with the poor, content ourselves with little, live in justice, and love mercy. He wanted parents to love their children and sons to honor their fathers. He honored me with his listening and his speaking the truth as he saw it.

He became more outspoken about preparing for a Messiah. Others would look at me with pity sometimes—a widow with one son who did not fit in. But I truly did not mind that. I knew him ever as a gift from God, and I trusted that the Almighty would somehow work through him. My part was to hold with open hands a space for seeking to know our God more deeply.

I knew those years were coming to an end when he told me he was ready for public ministry. He had never married—dedicated to God in a different way—and the fruit of that was coming clear. It was a spiritual reforming we needed, not a political one, he said. And he was called to prepare the way for the Messiah, the one who would come. He had a few followers with him, beyond the Jordan, and he was starting to baptize people. "A baptism of repentance," he told me, "a baptism that declared a turning to a new life, a life where God's ways were all that mattered." I gave him my blessing. I took his hands in mine and told him that it was for this he had been born—to turn the hearts of the fathers to their children, and the hearts of the children to their fathers, to the father of us all. He pointed to the gracious God of our ancestors, and our children's children. He looked at me with love, kissed me goodbye, and walked into the eye of the storm, the storm that never left him again.

I heard the stories: how many of the outcasts went and listened to him and were baptized by him and his disciples in the Jordan, how he preached to them and told them how to change their ways. Gradually, others went—the more well-to-do, even Pharisees and soldiers. I knew that his popularity could mean danger for him; I knew too that it would not stop him from speaking. The hardness that had been there when he was a young man had been tempered into fearless honesty.

"What are we to do?" people would ask him. He would look them in the eye and tell them the very thing. He would say: give away your riches, share your food with the poor, stop complaining about your wages, return what you have gained through injustice. I heard between the lines of the rumors that, while many admired his outspokenness, others thought he had gone too far. I wondered myself when he called the Pharisees a "brood of vipers." What would Zechariah have said to that? Zechariah, too, had spoken occasionally of his frustration at the hypocrisy of some of the religious leaders. But he would never have said it publicly as John was now. He was calling not just individuals to repentance but the whole nation. He called for our religious system to rightly represent a God of justice and mercy. I remember hearing what he had said and knowing they would not be able to listen—it would cost them too much. I also knew that he would not stop speaking now that he had started. Now that he knew the change it brought in people's lives, he would continue.

I wondered how it would end. Would the Pharisees stone him for blasphemy or draw a knife in the dark of a quiet desert night? I prayed to the God of our nation for the Messiah to come—as generations had prayed—but, I had to admit, my own prayer was so that my son would know his purpose fulfilled. Even as I prayed, I knew that it is never fulfilled. We all need to be called again and again to the ways of truth and justice.

Then the rumors came again, this time of one John had named, the Lamb of God. I understood why he chose that name from their talks with Zechariah of the deeper meaning of the feasts. The Passover lamb died so the people could go free, the blood spelled the remission of sins. I did not understand the full meaning then, only that John called him the Lamb and named him as the one who was to come.

Slowly more details trickled back. The Lamb was one Jesus of Nazareth who was going about teaching; indeed, bringing healing to the sick. I'd heard little of Jesus over those latter years. Mary would send a message through the family, but she herself did not always get to Jerusalem. She sent news, saying only that Jesus worked with his father in the carpenter's shop. I wondered at that, after the promise he had shown. But after John had gone I knew little of his life. Now, they said, he healed the sick, gave sight to the blind, and traveled with a band of followers preaching the good news, even as John did. But even in the rumors I could hear the difference. John called the people to repentance. Jesus, they said, went about doing good. Ah, Mary, I thought, may your son indeed do good; may he receive the love of the people and turn their hearts to a God of love.

Finally, I heard of John's arrest and imprisonment. Shocked though I was, I was not surprised. He would not soften the truth for anyone, not even for Herod. Of course we all knew Herod should not have taken his brother's wife. But we did not say it—not publicly, at least. But John ever believed the power of truth. All people needed in order to change was to be confronted, he seemed to say. Willing to pay a high cost himself to be right with God, he believed everyone else longed for that also. And he was half right. For a time Herod had kept him—kept him alive, so I heard—to listen to what he had to say. But the final outcome was inevitable. Prophets are killed by those in power. I knew it all his life. I hoped, of course, that he would be an exception. I hoped that the people whose lives he influenced would somehow protect him. He died, barely thirty, killed by a cowardly king.

Even as I grieved, I knew he fulfilled what he was born for, lived the life he was called to. I was grateful that he had served God in the way he believed and had turned the hearts of many to that God.

Mary came to me then. She was the age I had been when she first came, and I could see in her a deep knowing that she too would suffer this grief. I had not faced that possibility for Jesus. I was still hoping his was another way. Mary laid her hand on mine and reminded me that the Lamb of God gives his life so others may live. She said it with a tearful dignity. "I came," she said, "because I knew people would not understand. Even my own children think they're crazy sometimes—these sons of ours. But Elisabeth, you and I know. We know that the ways of God are deeper than our understanding. I came to remind you, as you reminded me, that though his ways are mystery and darkness at times, they are always love, always grace, always invitation to a higher way."

It was only later I realized that there were dark currents under the surface. There were those who threatened death for blasphemy, those whose lifestyle was disturbed by a call to true righteousness, those who rejected a God of grace if it meant forgiveness to the sinful. It wasn't long—only two short years— before Mary's son, too, was killed. He was killed for his refusal to silently hide the truth of a God in whom mercy and justice kissed each other, a God whose ways are so different from the religious rules. I have heard tell that some of you have seen him. It is beyond my old woman's imagining. And yet I believe. If the life of God can break through the rules of birth, so can that life break through the rules of death. Death cannot hold back that life.

Mary's Reflection

As Elisabeth spoke these last words, she stared into the distance. Then she turned her gaze to me. "So, my child, tomorrow you will tell me your story, and help me see this further unfolding."

Old, wise Elizabeth.

As I remember you speaking I am touched by your grace.

The grace of a mother who gave her son so generously—not once, but again and again.

I remember a woman who knew through and through that God is no man's debtor and that though God gives and takes away, God is still is to be trusted.

I was reminded of Hannah who promised her child to God before he was born, and then let him go after a few short years.

I was reminded of Job who lost all and still worshipped. Blessed be the name of the Lord.

I was reminded of Mary, who I knew so well, who also knew how to hold dear but then to surrender.

I watched Elisabeth's lined face as she remembered, saw the emotions enliven her eyes, and knew she was not one who lived in an unreal, pious religion. She was one who gave all and lost and gave again. She chose to trust God, at whatever cost, whatever others said. She found God to be enough for her.

So I told her my story, from my childhood in Magdala, through my long years of sickness, to my vital years of adventure, following the one I loved with all my heart. I told her of his torturous death and of that morning in the garden when I saw the glory of God infused in flesh. She listened intently to every word, sometimes asking for clarification, sometimes pausing to sit with me in silence as we pondered some story of joy or heartbreak. When I finished, I told her of my desire to gather together the stories of the Messiah. She laid her old clawed hand on mine, and spoke simply:

"Follow the threads of your story, child. They will guide you. And you, too, will weave a tapestry of darkness and light, and know the faithfulness of our God who will not leave you bereft."

I stayed with her another couple of days, waiting to join others heading for Jerusalem. I wanted to hear all I could from her, soak in her kindness, and remember as much as I could to relate to Mary when I next saw her. As I left, Elisabeth held me tightly, knowing it was unlikely we would meet again. I think she saw something in me of her own hopes and dreams—hopes carried into the next generation and dreams her son must have known as he longed for the transformation of a nation named after his God. I felt something of the responsibility then and pondered it as I walked the dusty roads back to the city. I carried the responsibility to listen well, both to our God and the people I would seek out. I must retell their stories faithfully, in order to tell the greater story of a God who comes to us.

I pondered who I might go to and how to weave together this tapestry of Jesus' life and the kingdom he spoke of so often. I let my mind run back over the previous years, seeing in my mind's eye the faces of those who had been healed, those who had offered us hospitality, and those who had journeyed with us. I thought of those who were there at the beginning of Jesus' ministry. Always conscious that some of the men would not appreciate what I was doing, I was still determined to be open to the Spirit's leading. I have tried to order the stories so they follow the course of Jesus' life, but that's not the way I heard them. Sometimes I met someone unexpectedly and as we spoke I would remember who they were. Sometimes they remembered me, and sometimes not. Always they were delighted to tell of their experiences and the deep, life-changing effect of their encounter with Jesus.

At the beginning though, as I made my way back to Jerusalem after hearing Elisabeth's story, I pondered how to tell Jesus' story. How would I find people who would help it all make sense for the ones who came later and hadn't seen anything of the ministry of Jesus? Maybe some wouldn't have even heard of his death and resurrection. Although I joined the disciples early in Jesus' ministry,

I was not there right at the beginning. I reminded myself of the stories of each of the men in Jesus' traveling band and how they had first met him.

3

A Fisherman and the Politics of Change

Andrew[1]

ANDREW HAD BEEN ONE of the first followers. I used to watch him sometimes as he listened to Jesus. I recognized in him the way of listening that I myself knew. A listening that wasn't all about action—as Peter was. Peter, as you have surely heard, was outspoken and impetuous. Andrew, his brother, was a slower, deeper thinker with a deep commitment. His listening was more about the heart, the meaning, the implications for an inner relationship with the God he knew from the sea, the stars, and the silence of being alone on the shore or the water. He was a solid, quiet man, Andrew. He took his time to respond, but he was always trustworthy when you needed him. I'd seen him throw in his lot with Peter or the other disciples, make the best of a challenge, go without. He wasn't one to complain. I'd see him watching and thinking. When some of the others were critical of me or wouldn't welcome my presence, he

---

1. John 1:29–46, Matt 4:18–19.

would always make a place for me. I think he caught something of my own deep longing for God's presence and respected that.

When I returned to Jerusalem I sought out Mary. She was living with us in those days, those early exciting years when we were all abuzz with what it meant to live the kingdom. Those of us from Jerusalem stayed with other believers. Many opened their homes to each other, their extended households extended further. We met together and shared the latest events: the healings, the new believers, the rising suspicions of the authorities. Once I had settled back and caught up with all that had been happening, I went looking for Andrew. I found him staying at the home of a new believer, helping a group of them understand the way of Jesus more deeply. I shared with him my idea of gathering stories. He smiled slowly, and his eyes took on a faraway look. "I'd love to talk about it, Mary. It will bring back those early times!"

Andrew's Story

We grew up in Bethsaida by the shores of Galilee. Our father, John, was a fisherman; being on boats was our daily life. From when we were little we would help. Our father, though rough around the edges, was a deeply kind man. We must have sometimes got around his feet. He seldom told us off, except out in the boats. There, you have to do what you're told and look sharp about it. Sometimes, in the water, it's a matter of staying in the boat or getting a sudden cold dip in the sea! I learned that one the hard way, not moving fast enough when a gust of wind came through, slipping off the side railing, and getting a dunking. Of course we'd learned how to survive in the water from when we were tiny; I could look after myself till they picked me up out of the water. It taught me to listen to my father and obey quickly.

Growing up a fisherman teaches you a lot about life and death and what's worth living for. Even though Galilee is not large—most of the time you can see from one side to the other—sudden squalls can come up without warning. Lives were lost often enough through my boyhood. Night fishing added the danger of not always having our bearings quite right. Since we knew life could come to a sharp end, we felt it was worth living to the full. My father demonstrated that with his joy and anger, his laughter and his reverence and his patience while teaching us boys. And fishing takes patience. Often you go home empty-handed and hungry. You have to trust the Creator God with your life or you'd easily live in fear. My father taught us that year after year.

He wasn't an educated man, my father, but he loved the God of the open heavens and sometimes bellowed out his praise to God when we were out on the water—as if the rush of joy couldn't be kept inside. Peter took after him a bit in that, and I loved it in them both, but that wasn't my way. Nevertheless, I learned to love this God of the sea and sky, the God of the stars and the soft evening light. My father would quote (or misquote) the psalms, with heartfelt passion. Even his anger and frustration would burst out with recognition that God was present. "And what, Jahweh, are you going to do about that?" he'd shout. He had no patience with the political situation and little respect for the Romans. I was glad enough more than once that he could vent his anger out on the sea where there were no Romans to hear and take offence at him. He didn't look to political answers for our nation, though; he laid all the responsibility on the God of Israel and would tell him so.

That's what made him interested in the prophecies about the Messiah, the other part of the scriptures he'd quote. "For unto us a child is born, unto us a son is given, and the government will be upon his shoulders." He loved, "His glory is from the rising of the sun, and he will come to Zion as a Redeemer." We were often out on the water as the sun rose and he loved to quote that one then. He would add, "And boys, you can be sure he will come. God will send us a Redeemer to get us out of this mess." That's where we brothers got our expectation, our conviction that a Messiah would come. And it was to our father's credit that he would encourage us to go, and leave him and our other brothers to look after the fishing, while we checked out another rumor about a Messiah. For some reason it was Peter—Simon as he was called when we were growing up—and I who were especially taken with this search. Simon-Peter was the oldest, married with a family of his own. Next came our brothers in their twenties; then me, the youngest, at nineteen. With a family like that I did a lot of listening and thinking—the stories of the Messiah would catch at my heart. I think for Simon-Peter it was more about changing the world. We would keep our ears open and share the gossip when the day's fishing was over.

News travels fast around boats. Sailing up and down the lake, the fishermen heard the news of travelers from Jerusalem and sailed it up to the other fishermen. The stories would get garbled, no doubt about that, but we'd know when something was astir. That's how we heard about John the Baptizer and his talk of preparing the way for someone greater. We'd talk about it at night as we sat together with other fishermen, mending our nets. How would we know the Messiah? He'd come and turn the Romans out for sure, some would say. He would come and rule as king in Jerusalem. No, he would raise an army of all the occupied nations and march on Rome. The stories got wilder and wilder. My father was all for a return to a kingdom of Israel, free of any Roman rule. I'd listen to the conversation and wonder. Even as a boy, I had the awareness of the almighty God present in the waves and the thunder. But I also loved the silence that would descend sometimes in the soft evening light or as dawn was bringing color to each tree on the hillside. I knew this God of silence, the God of transforming light; my heart would stir and call me to a God of inner places. I wondered what a Messiah of this God would look like. What if it wasn't about Roman rule, but about the inner heart, the way we were to live? How would I recognize this Messiah? Would my inner heart tell me or would I have to see some sign?

And what of this John the Baptizer? They said crowds were going to him down at the Jordan River, out from Bethany. Pharisees were going out to hear what he had to say. People were getting baptized for the repentance of sins. "See," said one of the fisherman, "it's the beginning of the raising of an army." Could this John be the Messiah? Apparently, he said he was preparing the way for someone else to come—what could this mean? The conversation would go back to Isaiah's words, "In the wilderness prepare the way of the Lord. And the glory of the Lord shall be revealed, and all flesh shall see it together. Speak tenderly to Jerusalem, and cry to her, that her warfare is ended." "There!" claimed one of the men, "How much more clear can you get? The Messiah will reign in Jerusalem and the whole Roman empire will see it."

But I was off on another tangent. My dreams were in another direction. I had heard "tenderly." I heard "speak tenderly to her," and again I felt the undercurrent of this God who draws the heart. The ache of tenderness drew me more strongly than any call to a conquering army. I wanted to go and find out firsthand what this Baptizer was saying.

We got our father to sail us down to the southern end of the lake where the Jordan carries the waters south. It wasn't difficult to follow the rumors and find the wild-looking John. He looked just like you'd expect an old-style, fiery prophet to look. Ragged hair, big beard, camel-hair cloak with a leather belt, and what a voice! I thought my father was rough around the edges. This John was as rough as they come—not so much in a rambunctious way, like my father, but in an absolute, no-compromise, demanding way. Sometimes he'd fix you with this steely look and you'd feel like he was searing your whole hidden heart with a fire-torch. Even so, Simon-Peter and I hung around. It's not as though he made us particularly welcome, but the way he spoke of the Messiah coming was so absolutely convincing. He was very clear that he himself was not the Messiah, but that the Messiah would come and John would recognize him. We almost expected to see him come down from the clouds in Elijah's chariot.

John would quote the scriptures we were all familiar with, but his favorite one was: "I am the voice of one crying in the wilderness. 'Make straight the way of the Lord.'" He would tell people in no uncertain terms how they needed to straighten out their lives. We tried to ask him when the Messiah was coming and what he would do, but in the end we were sure he didn't know. He often quoted another passage in Isaiah, too, that fit my wonderings about a Messiah of the heart, rather than of the army. "Surely he has borne our griefs and carried our sorrows. Like a lamb that is led to the slaughter." I questioned John on that one—what could it possibly mean? "Andrew, I don't know what it means, but you don't think the people will welcome him with open arms, do you? Not when he comes bearing fire. The Romans, the rulers, the Pharisees—they're not going to like the changes he brings."

Again, he couldn't really explain what the changes would be, but he had a total conviction that the Messiah was coming and that he, John, would know him when he came. "God has told me," he would say. Although I secretly wondered how God told him, I believed him when he said it. "God has told me I am not fit to undo his sandal strap, but that when he comes I will know, I will see the Spirit of God upon him and he will baptize you with the Holy Spirit." I tried to imagine seeing the Spirit of God, the breath of God, the wind. Maybe it would be like seeing the cloud the Israelites followed into the wilderness or Ezekiel's wheels within wheels. I lived those days in heightened expectation.

When it happened, it was much quieter and less dramatic. I may not have taken any notice except for John's total assurance. Simon-Peter wasn't even there. Had gone off to get supplies and left me with my daydreams and my watching for the Messiah. Afterwards, as I tried to go back over his coming, I wasn't even sure that I had seen the dove John claimed. It was common for birds to be around the riverbank. I like to think I did glimpse a flutter of Holy Spirit wings.

I was more conscious of the conversation John and this man were having out there in the water. Sometimes when there were crowds, we'd help with the baptisms. Sometimes, John would be shouting out to the people what they needed to do, "He who has two coats, let him share with him who has none; he who has food, let him do likewise." He tended to be short and sharp with people. That day, as I watched from the bank, I saw him in conversation with a man I had not seen before. The set of John's shoulders was much more like one asking for advice rather than dealing it out. I was curious to see something of a different manner even in the way he baptized him. It was as though he was treating him with deep respect.

John seldom treated people with great respect. It was sufficiently different for me to get up and go to John. Jesus—yes, of course it was him—was already walking away when I got to John. And John was looking after him with a distant look in his eye and a hushed voice: "He told me I would see the Spirit descend upon him and I did. I saw the Spirit descend as a dove from heaven, and it remained on him." He turned to me with his piercing eyes, "Did you see it, Andrew?"

I couldn't answer him; as we both turned, I tried to pick out which one he was as he disappeared into the crowd. "He's the one who baptizes with the Holy Spirit," he said in awe. It was so different from what I had expected. I just gazed after him, wondering what I was supposed to do. If Simon-Peter had been there I'm sure he would have done something. He would have run and fallen at his feet or something dramatic. I acted more slowly and ended up doing nothing except searching my heart for some flicker of recognition.

The next day, of course, I was back and never left John's side. "I'll tell you if he comes," he assured me. That was something I always admired in John: while such a commanding figure himself, he had no need of approbation. His total purpose was to prepare people for the coming of the Messiah, to point them to him, and to send them on their way. He continued to baptize and deal out his sharp advice, but I could see he was often glancing up to the banks.

At last he saw him. He stood tall and silent before proclaiming, "Behold, the Lamb of God!" For ever after, that's what I would remember when I thought about this fiery, rough, prophetic man—his deep reverence as he announced the enigmatic Messiah. "Behold, the Lamb of God!"

This time I was ready, and hurried up out of the water to follow him. He turned, looked at me, and said evenly, but with a hint of laughter, "What are you looking for?" I don't know what I was expecting, but it wasn't that. I stumbled out, "Rabbi, where are you staying?" "Come and see," he answered. And off we went, just like

that, as though it was commonplace to find a Messiah! He immediately began to speak of the kingdom that was coming and my
heart warmed as he spoke. Then he paused, "Andrew, what are you
looking for?" This time I managed a bit more. "John said you were
coming to change the world, that you would bring fire and justice."
He looked at me with a look I came to know well. It was a look inviting me to a deeper place of honesty and a deeper heart response.
I searched for the words to express what I had been pondering so
long. "I am looking for someone who will show us how to live as
though God is really present and loves us each tenderly, as though
it is possible to love mercy and to do justly." He smiled at me. I
knew he understood and that I could follow him. At last I was sure
enough of myself to ask him if I could come back. I explained to
him that my brother had also been looking for his coming. "Of
course," he said. I went off in search of Simon-Peter.

At last I found him, returning from his journey, and I told
him excitedly, "We have found the Messiah!" Simon-Peter only be-
lieves what he sees for himself, but he trusted me enough to come
directly. As we entered the house, Jesus looked at my brother with
that searching look and asked, "So you are Simon the son of John?
You shall be called Peter." Simon-Peter, for once in his life, was
stuck for words. It was only later he told me that he felt as though
his inner being was laid open. John the Baptizer seemed to search
for any hidden sin. Jesus saw all of that but looked for the deeper
possibilities, longings, and cherished hopes—and somehow called
them forth.

It took us a while to get to sleep that night, with the radical
possibilities stirring us to all sorts of speculation. At last we slept
and woke with the expectation of a new life beginning. Jesus wasn't
there. No one knew where he had gone. We hung around, fearful
he'd left us behind. Simon-Peter couldn't stand it and had to act,
so we went to find John the Baptizer. He listened to us and then
looked off into the distance. "He'll need to be alone," he said. "He'll
need to test it, to take it to God." Seeing our puzzled looks he said,
"Before I came here to call people to repentance, I spent many days
with God alone, testing my calling until I knew that what I felt

could be said publicly. He's been recognized publicly. Now he will need to be alone for a time. Go back home. God will guide you."

There was nothing else to do. We set off for Galilee, reviewing our old speculations. Of course, having met Jesus now, there was a totally different perspective. I was sure that the kingdom he spoke of had nothing to do with the Roman occupation. Simon-Peter wasn't so certain. "How can you have a new kingdom without replacing the old?" he countered. On we talked over the long miles until we reached the lake again. We found some boats that would help us homeward.

We reached home and told our father what had happened. I remember the look on his face as he listened to us. I knew then how deep was his longing for the Messiah. Before, I'd seen it as his answer for the chaos of our times, but now I sensed something of the deep longing I felt in my own heart. It was a longing not only for a better world but for a depth of relationship with a God who is intimately interested in our lives.

We didn't know then, but this was to be a pattern for the years that followed: challenging encounters with Jesus followed by times of returning to everyday life in Bethsaida—fishing, mending nets, swapping stories, and speculating. One day, weeks after we had come back, several of us were out on the shore casting the hand-nets out for the fish near the beach. Casting, dragging, casting, when suddenly, a voice called to us: "Follow me, and I will make you fishers of men." There he was—no explanation, just that look of deep invitation. Simon-Peter and I looked at each other, pulled in our nets, threw them to the others, and went with him.

Andrew paused and smiled at me. "You know how it was, Mary. Lots of others didn't understand. But for those of us who did, well, that invitation—it was worth everything."

Mary's Reflection

Andrew.
Dependable, quiet, thoughtful.
You watch and think and pray.

I see you sometimes, as we walk, the others arguing or questioning,

And you—listening, coming to your own conclusions, saying little.

You became one to whom others came.

Wary of your louder brother, unsure of the others,

They would come to you, the quiet one, and ask for help, ask about Jesus.

And you would bring them, claiming no knowledge in yourself.

You would turn to Jesus, turn to God the Father and seek a way.

Thank you, Andrew, for your quiet strength.

Thank you for including me,

In your rough but gentle way.

Andrew went on to include many others, introducing them to a God who came for the outcasts, the little people, the outsiders. He knew himself as a man unlearned, but one who knew his God—and that was all that mattered to him.

After he had told his story, Andrew and I continued to speak of others we had encountered along the way. Some he had met again since; he knew where I could find them. He became something of a companion to me as I sought people out and returned to recount what they had told me. There he would be—solid, encouraging, always interested in my journeys and my encounters. A few times he traveled with me, especially if I needed a protector, and always he was there when I returned to share my encounters.

4

Deep Thirst, Deep Quenching

The Woman at the Well[1]

ONE OF THE EARLY stories of Jesus' ministry centers on the little town of Sychar in Samaria. Most of us didn't like to go that way from Jerusalem to Galilee because the Samaritans were generally inhospitable, even hostile. The old history of them not being "pure" Jews alienated them from us, and us from them. But this particular time Jesus chose to go that way. He had been in Judea where some of the disciples had been baptizing and he was returning to Galilee. It was before I had joined them, but they told the story another time when we traveled that way. I had briefly met the woman at the center of the narrative. As the story goes, it was noon and they were hungry and hot. On the way into the village they passed a well in the shade of some trees. If there had been something to draw water with they would have stopped for a drink before going into the village. But there was nothing except a low stone wall around the well-opening—enough to keep animals

1. John 4:4–42.

31

from falling in—and a few scruffy trees. They continued walking, but Jesus dropped back, "You go on and get some food," he said. "I need some time by myself."

He sank down in the shadiest spot and they thought he might be asleep in moments. As they came near the village, a woman passed them, carrying a water jar. Her scarf shadowed her face and she averted her eyes. They noticed even then that she pulled away from them. They went into the town and found a marketplace where they took a while to haggle over prices. Though they knew they were being taken advantage of as outsiders, they finally found enough for a meal and some food for later in the day. There was no knowing where they might get to before nightfall. They made their way back to the well, expecting the woman to be long gone and Jesus to be asleep under the trees. Instead, as they came close, they saw the woman, bold as brass, in deep conversation with Jesus, the water jar on the ground between them.

Neither of them turned as the men came up. It was only as they set the food down that she finally turned and looked at them, realizing they were with Jesus. She turned back to Jesus and laughed a laugh of such joy, they told me later. Then she left, telling them to wait until she had brought her friends.

As they ate, Jesus told the men of the conversation. They noticed how refreshed he was. It was as though he had drunk deeply, not just of water but of friendship. They stayed some days in that village, and the hostility they had encountered turned to welcome as more and more of the townspeople heard Jesus' teaching.

It was only years after I had begun gathering stories that I remembered the town and what had happened there. I wondered what had become of the woman. Had the acceptance she had begun to receive from the villagers continued? Did her recognition of the Messiah truly transform her life? On one of our journeys back to Galilee, I persuaded my companions to take the route through Sychar so we could seek her out. Once we got there it wasn't difficult to find her: she had clearly become a legend in the place.

The Woman at the Well—The Samaritan Woman's Story

You ask me to tell you the story of my encounter with Jesus and how it changed my life. Well, it totally transformed it! In those days I was a bitter, angry woman. I neither expected anything of the world nor gave anything back. I had learned survival by then and woe betide anyone who got in my way. I lived with a man I did not care for simply for the protection he gave. I had no friends. The townsfolk had no time for me nor I for them. I avoided them, ignored their snide remarks, and kept to myself.

When Jesus appeared one day, I treated him like everyone else. I expected contempt and rejection and I gave it first. What I remember most about Jesus was how he refused to be put off by my sarcasm. He could somehow hold the pain of my life without flinching. He was not afraid of my anger or my inner torment—he just held a space for me to be who I was. You've probably heard something of my past life. Even in those days I was known as a woman with a past. Most people know I've had five husbands and, until they get to know me, I get these knowing looks. It doesn't bother me now, but once upon a time I was like a powder keg, reacting to every sly look, every muttered remark. The deep healing that started that day hasn't changed who I am, but it's certainly given me peaceful ways of relating. Now, I'm part of a loving community. What a gift!

Yes, you could certainly say I have a colorful past—not the colors I'd be choosing if it was me doing the painting, either! But then, in a way, you mustn't regret the past. It's what has made me who I am. And who knows, if I'd had an ordinary life I may never have met the extraordinary man who changed my blacks and greys and blood reds into blues and golds, laughter and joy. Oh, not that it's all been joyful and sweet! I've had my share of hard learning to do, calloused layers to be scraped away, anger and bitterness to be dissolved and re-dissolved. But life has been rich and, truly, looking back I wouldn't swap it for anything. I've found the God who is Father to us—and that is worth everything.

Let me go back to the beginning and tell you something of the journey that brought me to be the angry, tormented woman who met Jesus. I've wondered if it was my father who set me on the wrong track in the first place. Not that you can blame him. Everyone makes their own choices, but my father's choices certainly helped shape me into the woman I am, even today. "A hard woman" some people have called me: sharp of tongue, shrewish, "a Jezebel." I laugh it off these days, but I wasn't always able to.

My father was part of all that. He was heavy-handed with us children and with my mother on occasion. That's what got me into trouble—I began to answer him back, to defend her or the little ones. It just got me more blows. I think even then I had a strong sense of justice and a sense that a God of justice would not allow evil to triumph. So I felt vindicated in standing up to my father. It didn't make for a happy home. When they tried to marry me off at the first chance, well, I was glad to go.

My first husband was a kind young man. He didn't know what to make of me sometimes with my angry outbursts, but we got on well enough. I realize, looking back, that I really hardly had time to know him. And I've wondered if my comparing all men with him ever since is a childish romance. I will never know the answer to that. He came from a religious family; his talk of a Messiah fired my imagination. He used to tell me that a Messiah would come to set the world to rights. I used to listen to the stories and prophecies with wonder.

But that got pushed into the background when I became preoccupied with my pregnancy. Then our little daughter was born. It was the year when that awful plague came through. My husband was one of the first to die. I was taken in by his brother, as our custom is, but his wife had disliked me from the first. It didn't help that I'd taken it upon myself to sort her out on a few matters in the short time we'd known each other. Now she was especially resentful. When this husband too was taken by the plague—whole families were wiped out with it—I determined to get away from that family. I questioned where the God of justice and his Messiah were then. Yet I think even in that, I had a sense that calamity and disaster didn't prove there couldn't be a good God. Maybe it was even something of that faith that gave me hope to try and start my life over with someone new.

Foolish, really, when you think about it: a young child, a woman alone. But, I'm a pretty stubborn one and I thought I could find someone else. I did too, a man who had been widowed (a lot of deaths there were in that year). It didn't take me too long to realize that he was worse than my father. Oh, he was fine some of the time, but then he'd drink and get really mean with it. I put up with it for a long while, afraid of what would happen to me and my little one. At first I'd try and reason with him when he was sober and he'd promise, remorseful and contrite, to mend his way. My sense of justice would get the better of me when he didn't follow through. I'd scream and rant at him. He'd bellow back at me that of course he could control his drink. But then, the next feast day, he would be drunk again. I put up with it, until the day he hit my daughter. Some small childish thing she'd done: tripped over her own feet and knocked my husband's cup of wine over. The blow she got slammed her against the wall. My own black eyes I could put up with, but not this, not the abuse of the sweet light of my life. I didn't know what to do. There was no way I would go back to my father, nor to my first husband's family. I took off in the night with my daughter and the little I could carry. I begged food, and, yes, I sometimes paid for it with my body—what did it matter if only I could get away?

Finally I came to a town where I knew no one. I'd thought up a story by then. I told them I'd fled from a raid of Roman soldiers, lost my husband who had died trying to protect me, suffered rape but managed to escape. I think even in that I was trying to invent a noble husband, someone who would give his life for me, a Messiah of my very own. The townsfolk were kind enough to take me in. But what can you do with a woman alone, no family, and a child to care for? When an older man offered to have us, to marry me, it was better than prostitution. There were no other alternatives.

Gradually, he worked out the truth. My daughter, in her innocence, said a few little things. And I said things I shouldn't—yes, my sharp tongue again—and he somehow worked out that my last husband was still alive. In a way, it was in his interests to keep it quiet, but he used it to blackmail me. I grew to hate him, but he gave us a roof over our heads while my daughter grew up a little. I can't say it was much of a marriage, but, until he died, I looked after him, physically at least, in exchange for his name and his roof.

I determined then that I would somehow stay alone. I'd grown to know people in the town. Surely I could help out in lots of ways—enough to get food for the two of us. It worked for a while. My daughter, at nine, was old enough by now to help me. A real pretty little thing she was by then—she was probably the one who got us any good will, truth be told.

She was the one who got me my last husband too, though I didn't realize it till later. He was another widow, his wife not long dead from childbirth, with two other little ones. When he asked me to marry him, I thought it would give us a family to belong to. How could I be so blind? He was worse than any of them. Oh, charming he could be—and maybe that romantic longing blinded my eyes to what I should have sensed in him. Even in the short time I was with him, I began to feel really uneasy about him. I'd put it down to my own mistrust—I hadn't had a lot of practice in trusting.

I got busy being a wife and mother of a family in a way I'd never done in my life. Then one night, I'd gone to bed early, tired from the busy day and the constant needs of the little ones. Some sound woke me from a bad dream, as it happened. My husband was not in the bed and some instinct told me to check on my daughter where she slept with the little ones. She wasn't there. Panicked, I ran outside. He had her in a dark corner, her young body naked in the glimpse of moonlight. I screamed and tore at him, all the vile words of the vile years pouring out. He grabbed me then, his big hand over my mouth. He pulled my head close to his mouth and swore by heaven and hell that if I said a word to anyone he would tell them what he knew of my past. "Oh, yes, I know," he said. "Old Elias wasn't that good at keeping secrets. There isn't a man in this town that doesn't know what a whore you are. You say a word of this and I'll soon set them straight on who the liar is." He pushed me to the ground and left me, assured that he could win every round. I went to my daughter and huddled myself against her. Finally, she slept in my arms and I sat there long, deciding what to do. How could I have come to this? How could I have trusted a man after all I knew? I hated my gullibility; I hated myself. I was frozen by those venomous words.

In the darkest hours, I escaped. I actually carried my sleeping daughter out of the house, deathly afraid of waking anyone. I dare say, though, my husband would have let me go anyway. What future could there be? Unless he really did think he could force me into silence and submission. Still, I could take no risks of anything other than flight. I took only a cloak for warmth and set out looking for another town, another life.

What else can I tell you of my former life? I still hardly speak of what followed before I came to Sychar. What I had lied about came upon me. In our haste through the dark countryside, I stumbled into a band of men sleeping around a burnt-out fire. They raped us, my precious daughter and I, and left us for dead in a ravine. She never recovered. Somehow, I did recover and found my way to Sychar where another man put a roof over my head. I brought in what money I could and, in exchange, he provided me a place to live and a male to protect me. Neither of us bothered to call it a marriage.

Slowly, I got some of the old fight back, but life was very bitter. I expected no God to rescue me from the hell I lived in now; I thought every last imagination of a Messiah had died within me. It was into that harsh reality that God sent me a Savior. I remember the day when I met him. Oh, yes! I've gone over it so many times in my mind, remembering every word he said and how he looked at me. I remember, too, how I answered him back and what I was like in those cruel days!

I'd gone down to get water, hot in the midday sun. I'd slept in again—the only escape I had from my life. I'd set off, finally, trudging through the dust and glare, bad-tempered and out of sorts. I got to the well at last, only to see a stranger, a Jew, sitting there. I didn't look at him. I didn't need another man to contend with, any further contempt to ward off. So I turned away from him as I made to let down my water jar. But I felt him looking at me. Just another man eyeing me up and down, so I thought. I turned abruptly to outstare him. Instead of the silent scorn I expected, he looked me straight in the eye and asked me for a drink. No condescension, just a simple request: "Give me a drink."

I had no patience with any man in those days, especially one I expected to turn on me in the next breath. Besides, I was so used to dealing in sarcasm that it came easily to my tongue. "How is it that you, a Jew, ask a drink from me—a Samaritan. A Samaritan *woman.*" I emphasized the woman, baiting him. I thought I knew what to expect of men, despised them before they had a chance.

But he came right back at me without scorn, without contempt, straight back, look for look, word for word. "If you knew the gift of God, and who it is that asks, you would have asked him, and he would have given you living water." That stopped me—it was the way he said it right in my face, but with no malice, no bravado, no score to settle. And, as I stared at him, I noticed how bone weary he looked. It was a feeling I knew too well: not just physical weariness, but the wrung out exhaustion of psychological battles. Nevertheless he stood, gently took the water jar out of my hands, and let it down into the well. I still said nothing as he drew it up and made to pour the water into my hands. I drank, took it from him and poured some for him.

His words and manner had floored me, but there was no way I would let down my guard with anyone. I stated the obvious, and let my usual sarcasm lace my words. "Sir, you have nothing to draw with and the well is deep. Where would you get this living water?" Already, I think I began to wonder if he was more than the exhausted man he looked, but still it didn't stop my taunting, "Are you greater than our father Jacob who gave us this well and drank from it himself, he and his livestock?" I found myself wanting to prove I was as good as they are, as good as these Jews who claim a direct line from God. We too are Jacob's offspring.

Again he came straight back at me, but not like most men I've dealt with: bullying, intimidating, or at least patronizing in their self-righteousness and smug superiority. No, he spoke directly to my heart, ignoring the superficial argument. "Whoever drinks of this water," he said, "will get thirsty again. But whoever drinks of the water I'm talking about will never thirst. The water I give is a fountain forever springing up into everlasting life."

What an outrageous claim. I could have laughed him to scorn then, and usually I would have, but he had this way of speaking that was like no man I had ever known. He spoke truth, right back at me, yet somehow respectful. It is hard to describe to anyone who has never met him. But there was still no way would I soften myself with any man—even this one. So I shot back at him, "Well, give it to me then!" And I did laugh, a bitter laugh. "Then I wouldn't have to come here. I wouldn't have to be thirsty, wouldn't have to haul up this water."

For a moment it was as though we both knew we were talking of a different kind of water, a different sort of thirst. And he was right on to me, calling my bluff: "Go and call your husband, then, and come back."

No way. No way was I going down that track and letting him see the creep of a man I now lived with. I would not let him see how far I'd fallen. So I snapped back at him, "I have no husband."

But this Jesus, he gave no quarter. He'd glimpsed the tiniest hint of my longing and he wasn't going to let go that easily. Look for look he gave, right down to my hidden heart. He'd sat down again and he was looking up at me, kind of stern, but compassionate, too. And as he sat in still silence, I felt as though he was taking my measure, maybe wondering how far he could push me.

I nearly turned away then, flaring into anger, hurting, thinking him the same as other men, after all. I was afraid he was treating me as something to be played with. But just as I broke his gaze, he spoke very quietly: "You're right in saying you have no husband. You've had five husbands and the one you are living with now is not your husband. You're speaking the truth about that."

I stared at him, all my anger welling up. There I was—exposed again, blamed again, belittled again. I wanted to snarl at him, tell him where to go with his clever tricks, except—except what? I've pondered often what it was that held me. There was something in the way he spoke that let me know he wasn't blaming or belittling me. He was simply speaking the truth and expecting the same of me.

The best I could do was resort to sarcasm again. "Sir, I perceive you are a prophet," I said; at least I didn't walk away. I knew now I wanted something from him, even though I couldn't say what. I tried to come up with something to ask him. Thinking I might provoke him, I brought up the old quarrel between the Jews and the Samaritans. "Our fathers worshipped on this mountain, and you Jews say Jerusalem is the place to worship."

He refused to be drawn; he didn't even give the usual Jewish rejoinder. Somehow he again connected with my deeper question. "Woman, believe me, the hour is coming when neither here nor in Jerusalem will you worship the Father." The Father? What was this? To speak of God as though he knew him. Who did this man think he was? He paused and watched my face with that measuring look. "You worship what you do not know; we know who we worship, for salvation is from the Jews." He paused again. I think he wondered if I would bite, if I would fight him and claim superiority. But this time I didn't. He said it so factually: "We know who we worship." There was no patronizing, just a statement. And if I was honest, I would have to admit I didn't know this God we were discussing, and I certainly wouldn't have used the word Father as he did.

He spoke slowly as if choosing his words carefully. "But the hour is coming, and is here, when the true worshippers will worship the Father in spirit and truth, for the Father is seeking such to worship him." I felt included in the "true worshippers," as if he had looked into my secret heart and seen my longing to find a God worthy of true worship. A God who is seeking? A God who is searching to find someone like me? I felt something in my heart melting. For there it was—as clear as any teaching I'd heard in my life—all in one sentence. To find a God worth being called God, all I needed was to be totally honest and totally true to this stirring I felt in my heart. And then, why then, I could find a God who could be called Father. A part of me felt totally exposed. I was called out in to the open for all to see, and yet, at the same time, I felt led into a secret so profound that all the world would want to know it. Watching my face intently, he spoke again, "God is Spirit, and those who worship him, must worship in spirit and truth."

I felt my masks slipping away. There was nothing I would hold on to in the face of this possibility of a God who asked nothing except truth. A God who had no requirements, no legalities, no straight-and-narrow righteousness—could this possibly be what God is like?

I could hear people coming up the path, but I didn't care; I didn't want this conversation to be over. It was my turn to look deeply and to search for the right words. "I know the Messiah is coming one day and when he comes he will explain all these things to us."

He didn't break my gaze, and he was not distracted by the men coming up behind me. He simply held my look and made another earth-changing claim: "I am he."

I stared. My head was tumbling with questions, possibilities, and the beginnings of real hope, hope I had not felt in years. But it was too late. A band of men and women were all around us saying it was time to eat, wanting to share what they'd brought. I finally pulled my eyes away, glanced at the group, and watched them settle down to eat. I realized that Jesus was one of them. But he was still looking at me. Clumsily I pushed the water jar at him. "Here," I said, "you'll be needing more water—and something to draw it with. And don't go away!" I was half laughing, half crying. "I'm going to do what you told me. And I'll be right back!"

And that's my story—well, just the beginning of it. But you know the rest: how half the town followed me out to see him and came to faith, how's there's still a group of believers here forming a community that's lasted all these years. And you know how my life was changed, totally turned upside down. Oh, not that I will ever make a sweet, gentle old lady. I've still got a sharp tongue if I need it, but the awful bitterness is gone and the sarcasm with it. And I don't have to hide my heart anymore—I've become one of the ones looking out for others with a broken heart, others who have lost their way and need to find the living water. Even the ones with addictions and secret vices—we try to welcome them and work with them. I'm known as the tough old crone that takes them in with open arms but gives them a straight word if they need it. Most of us need that: the word of the Father God who holds justice and mercy in his outstretched hands.

Mary's Reflection

As she finished her story, she turned and looked at me. "So you traveled with him," she said. "I envied the men who could travel with him. But it was clear that I was to stay here in Sychar. And already, even in those first few days, people were beginning to look at me differently, and I began to feel at home in a way I had not for years. So I stayed, and glad I am for that. We really have become a community of believers."

I marveled at that. Of course, there were communities in Jerusalem and in many other towns and villages, but this was one little town where Jesus had stayed for a few days, years ago. The transformation was not in just one life, but in the way a whole village lived. The presence of the Spirit was evident in them as it was also amongst us. It shouldn't have surprised me: God was at work in anyone who turned to him and, maybe even more so, among those who are excluded, rejected, and marginalized.

5

Exclusion Turned to Grace

The Syrophoenician Woman[1]

THE SAMARITAN WOMAN WAS not only alien to me, a Jew, but she also had been an outsider in her community. This made me remember another outsider, the one we called the Syrophoenician woman. I was part of the group of men and women traveling by then. We had been ministering in the towns around the Sea of Galilee and had been questioned by the Pharisees and scribes. Jesus decided we all needed a break. We traveled further north to the district around Tyre.

As we were walking, a woman caught up with us and asked for a drink from our water bags. I remember noticing her accent was different, but I was in some conversation and didn't take much notice of her. She stayed behind resting and only caught up with us again later in the day. After a while some of the others began to be annoyed, as she kept asking for help. Peter and one or two of the others took it on themselves to protect Jesus from the constant demands, and they told her to go away. She might drop back for a

1. Mark 7:24–30, Matt 15:21–28.

time, but then she would catch up with us at our next resting place and beg again for help. I remember looking from her pleading face to Jesus one of those times, but he simply ignored her. I was confused when he did this sometimes, but he had stated very clearly that we were having time away from people's needs. I waited to see what would happen.

The story that she eventually told us was painful and raw. But what stood out most strongly in my memory was how she answered Jesus and how he eventually listened to her as he would an equal. As I remembered her persistence, I wanted to see if I could find her and hear the story of an outsider teaching the Master.

The Syrophoenician Woman's Story

You knew me as the Syrophoenician woman, you say. In fact, my parents were Greek, my father a scholar who had been hired to educate the sons in a Roman household in Tyre. I was born in Tyre and so grew up speaking Hebrew, but my parents spoke to me in Greek. So I was always an outsider, always different, almost always excluded. It was only later, when I developed the healing skills, that I began to be needed and then grudgingly included for what I could give. Oh, it's a wearying thing to be always on the outside, always overlooked, left to last.

Maybe it was the unconscious awareness of my own foreignness that gave me a soft spot for those who are on the edges. Even as a child I'd notice the beggars. When I was very little there was an old beggar on a street corner near the markets. While other people hurried by, pretending interest in some pressing errand, I would stare. My mother would always find some small thing to give while I would examine the wizened face, the twisted limb, the sightless eyes. My mother would then take my hand and draw me away, making some comment about how we should share what we had. Perhaps that's what first drew my interest to helping the sick and gave me a desire to relieve suffering. Not that I did any of that as a child, but I seemed to notice exclusion and alienation. I saw the unfairness in the responses of most people who preferred to reject rather than include.

As I got older I became more conscious of my own difference. My father spoke to me in Greek, as I said, but he also taught me logic. He would explain ideas and mathematical concepts to me and question me about what I might be learning. He taught me to reason and to debate. I remember my mother once chiding him, only half in jest, that he shouldn't teach me to argue so well. I think I had just managed to win some argument with her and she'd given in about something, weary of my disputing.

Of course there was no place for a girl with an education and an ability to argue, but my interest in helping the sick led me to a wise-woman, a healer with herbs and medicines. I'd taken a fancy to a woman my mother knew, old Rebekah. She used to tell me stories of her childhood and explain the religious feasts and observances to me. I remember loving the story of Judith who saved the people of Israel with her clever arguments and deception of Holofernes. I think I wanted to be a bit of a Judith myself, saving the people with my skill and cleverness. Perhaps I thought I would finally be accepted by everyone if only I were clever enough.

Anyway, Rebekah had pains in her joints and, as she got older, she walked with difficulty. I would fetch her food from the markets or take plates of food from my mother's kitchen. One day, when I got there, she was sitting with a stranger. I started to leave, but she called me back. "This is Anna," she said, "you might learn something from her." Anna had made some hot compresses and placed them on Rebekah's joints. I smelled herbs and spices, and I saw that the pain lines in Rebekah's face were lessening. I listened with interest as Anna explained that while the heat brought some relief, particular herbs eased pain as well. She left me a few little packages and explained the basics of preparation.

It was months later that I met her again. The herbs she had left had long been used up. I tried to replace the spices from the markets and had even begun to visit gardens where someone might be growing the different herbs. Then one day Anna was at Rebekah's again. As she mixed some ingredients for a tonic, she told me of other people she helped. My fascination for healing began then and has continued ever since. Whenever Anna came to the city, Rebekah would call someone to fetch me; I accompanied her to visit sick people as often as I could. Although people were still suspicious of me, my being with Anna helped them accept me. I began to see that in this role I might have recognition.

Anna would also talk to me about other aspects of healing. She showed me how to touch with respect and gentleness. She even told me of prayers she would speak silently as she gently massaged a limb or wound a bandage. I could see that for her, healing was not just physical. I realized that the very person she was, brought peace and restoration. I didn't know if I could follow her in that. My religion was not the same as hers, and my clever tongue was more likely to bring strife than peace. But I tried to follow her wisdom, and she, for her part, recognized and encouraged my intentions.

Of course that was all years ago. Rebekah died and Anna appeared less and less often, so I had to develop my own skills. I was always on the lookout for remedies for sickness and would ever be asking those who traded in herbs and spices what they knew. I would find out about others who were gifted in this area and question them as much as they would allow. Gradually, I became something of a healer myself, and it did earn me a grudging respect. People include you, if they need you enough.

My healing role also gave me the chance to use my skills in arguing. Often, some sick person would be given the worst medicines. Someone else might be kept in darkness when what they needed most was sunlight. I became something of an advocate for those in distress, demanding what they needed with all the authority I could muster. That didn't always win me friends, but I didn't care, if only I could bring some relief for pain.

The point of all of this is that, when I needed most of all to be able to bring healing, I wasn't able to do anything. I've jumped ahead in the story, but this is where your Jesus comes into it all. I married, birthed three children, and continued to practice my healing as they grew up. It wasn't a good marriage—you don't get the best when you're an outsider— and he stuck around only until he thought he had a better deal working in the ships that came in and out of Tyre. I lived with some of his relatives, who rather resentfully allowed us to stay in their extended household. I managed to look after the children with gifts people gave me in gratitude for my skills. Our lives were bearable. Sometimes that meant leaving the children largely to look out for themselves, with, perhaps, a sharp word from another adult to keep them quiet.

Then, the worst that can happen befell us. I was out one evening, helping with a difficult birth. I was trying to keep the mother from too much pain as the birthing dragged on and on. At last her baby was born and I hurried home through the streets, guiltily hoping my own children had managed to eat and put themselves to bed. When at last I let myself into our shared room, I was horrified to find my son and older daughter huddled together in a corner. Their faces were streaked with blood and tears and their eyes were large and fearful. They flinched at every sound. When they saw me, my daughter started sobbing and my son, in broken sentences, finally told me the garbled story.

The three of them had somehow heard of a ship coming in, down at the docks. They knew I would have forbidden them to go, but they must have decided their father was on the ship or heard someone promise a traveling band of jugglers or puppeteers—I never did get to the bottom of that. Anyway, they promised each other it would be just to have a look and they'd be sure to be back home before I returned.

My little one, little Petra, my curly-haired darling, followed them in whatever they suggested. It all went well at first. They had gone down to the docks and, sure enough, they saw that a big foreign ship was in. They couldn't find any traveling band and, before long, realized they had stayed longer and gone further than they meant to. When they finally started back, little Petra was tired and they had to take turns carrying her. They had just set her down and were arguing about whether to take a dark lane—a shortcut, my son insisted—when round the corner came a group of sailors laughing and cursing and, obviously, having had too much to drink.

One of the men made a grab at my older daughter and my son jumped to her defense, fighting off a sailor who was snatching at her. Finally, she had got free and he yelled at her to run. When he turned to pick up Petra, she was nowhere to be seen. Some of the men had disappeared, but the one he had been fighting caught him off guard and downed him with a blow in the face. By the time he pulled himself to his feet again, the men had gone and so had both of his sisters. Hoping desperately that his sister had picked up little Petra, he stumbled home to find my older daughter sobbing and trembling alone. He was trying to find out anything she had seen when I arrived. I quickly bathed her face, tried to calm her, and left her to sleep with a neighbor.

My son then led me back to where the sailors had caught them. I carried a burning brand from the fire, partly for protection and partly for light. At last we came to the dark lane and I held the torch high as we entered. My first reaction was utter relief as I saw my darling Petra curled up against a wall. Then, cold fear, as I saw her eyes staring and I thought her dead. I caught her up in my arms—I will always remember that moment as I felt her warm little body press against mine—but her eyes just kept staring and she made no sound at all.

We hurried back through the dark streets, my son holding the torch and me hugging Petra close. I was trying to soothe both of them. Over the next two weeks, Petra spoke not one word. I tried all the remedies I knew, I bathed her little bruised body, I sang to her, I even tried to pray the prayers old Anna had spoken long ago. She lay on the bed, staring, sometimes shaking or crying silently, jumping with fear whenever anyone entered the room. At last, she began to look into my eyes instead of right through me. But she would not speak. Then she began to cry out in the night, to say words she should never have heard, let alone learned to say. Sometimes, during the day, her face would twist and her eyes would look through us again. I knew she was seeing things that had happened to her. Sometimes she laughed in a way that made my hair prickle; I began to fear we would never get her back.

She lay listlessly on the bed, eating nothing unless I fed it into her mouth myself.

How ironic that I, a healer and advocate, could not heal my own daughter. Hers was a sickness I could not touch. In desperation I began to visit those I knew who had healing arts. I tried everything they suggested. Then, I asked them for others who might know what to do. I only became more and more desperate. I had to admit that what had happened to my little girl had twisted her mind, had put a curse on her that I knew not how to shift. My son and older daughter were deeply affected also, but I had to leave them again and again to seek yet another person who might bring relief.

Finally, I heard rumors of one Jesus. He healed all who came to him, they said. I was skeptical of that and worried further, because my daughter's sickness was of the spirit and mind, not of the body. I had to admit that her strange laughter, her perverse words, her staring, fearful look spoke of an unclean spirit—one that I could neither soothe out of her, nor command from her.

This Jesus, I heard, was in our region with a band of followers. He was kind, they said, authoritative and deeply compassionate. Following the rumors, I finally found him, heading north from Galilee. He was none of these things. He simply ignored me. He and his followers had been resting in the scrappy shade of a few thorny trees. As I arrived, hot from the journey, he got up and proposed that they continue. He glanced only briefly at me and resumed the journey. One of the women gave me a drink of water as I sank down to a rock, and then she too went on; I was left behind in tears of frustration. After a rest and a struggle with despair, my determination returned. I got up to follow the cloud of dust I had been watching as they headed to the next village. When I reached the village I asked for them and found where they were staying. But no one would let me in. I gathered they were trying to rest from the busy weeks of healing and preaching around Galilee.

I found lodging for the night and caught up with them the next morning. That day, I walked with them and waited for an opportunity to speak with him. But Jesus again ignored me, talking quietly to the men walking with him. I was used to being slighted; I was long familiar with exclusion. But this did not fit with what I had heard of the compassionate healer or with my own practices as a healer. As I walked along with the group, I heard them tell of miracles they had seen and of arguments with Pharisees. I heard talk of a God who is Father. I began to think that my being a foreigner, and my religious beliefs were being held against me yet again. These men must be sectarian and exclusive, just like everyone else. I dropped behind, alternating between anger and despondency as I thought of my little girl, locked in her world of trauma and tormented by a demonic spirit.

I began to think I must just head home again, back to my children, to do the best I could for them. I thought of the many people I had helped, the times I had been out late at night, the times I had gone without food to stay with someone dying or in distress. And these were not my people either! But *I* had shown compassion, *I* had responded to their needs! My anger resurfaced and I determined to make him listen to me. I caught up with them again as they came near to another village in the late afternoon. Afraid they would find another place for the night and shut the door against me, I called out, "Lord, Son of David, have mercy on me." One of the men turned, but they all just kept walking. I cried out again, half running to catch up: "Son of David, have mercy on me!"

When I caught up with one of the women, lagging behind the men as they strode toward the houses, I told her, "My daughter is suffering terribly from demon-possession." She looked at me with some kindness, saying she would see what she could do, but that they were trying to get away from the needs and the crowds. She didn't give me much hope and some of the others turned and glared at me. We reached the hamlet of houses and, as I feared, they entered a house and shut the door against me.

Again I considered heading for home, but the thought of my little girl fired my determination. I stood outside, crying out to him: "Jesus, Son of David, have mercy on me! Have mercy on my little girl! Have mercy!" It seemed there was nothing left in the world for me to do except to stand at the door and cry over and over, "Have mercy! Have mercy!"

At length the door was opened. I was led inside. Even as I entered, I heard one of the men say, "She won't listen to us. You'll have to tell her. Send her away."

He looked at me. Though I could glimpse some kindness in his eyes, his face was not open. Before he could speak, I fell on my knees before him, again pouring out my litany: "Son of David, have mercy on me. My daughter has an unclean spirit. Please have mercy. Heal my little girl." He waited patiently until I paused. He invited me to sit down. Then he began to explain what they had been doing, traveling to the different villages around Galilee. Now they were taking time aside. "And," he said, "I was sent only to the lost sheep of Israel." There it was, the never-ending barrier was drawn. You are outside, we are inside. You cannot come in.

"But sir," I argued, "I have lived here all my life, bringing what little healing I can to the people who live around me. I do not decide to whom I will go based on their religion, birthplace, or nationality. I go to them because they are sick and they need my help."

He answered patiently but firmly, his eyes on mine, "I have to choose who I will spend time with: the lost ones who want an answer, the sick ones who want to be well. I go to the lost sheep of the tribe of Israel, those who have some understanding of the Father but miss the key understanding of his love. My time is for those so caught in law and judgment and punishment that they feel themselves excluded from the God who is all Love."

"But now you are excluding me!" I argued. "Can't you see the injustice of that? How can this be a God of love you are serving? I, too, need your help. Lord, please help me. Help my little girl."

He paused, but I could see I had not persuaded him. "It is not right to take the children's bread and toss it to their dogs," he said. I imagined the picture he had drawn. A family gathered together around a table. A loving father broke the bread and gave it to the children. A mother spooned stew from a pot. This family loved and cared for each other. And some dogs waited, knowing they would not receive the children's food. My children were excluded from that loving family. My children were not part of the generous bounty. Well, so be it. I still held my ground. I imagined a God who might be like that loving father, a God who might be kind enough to have dogs in his home. I imagined some little dogs under the table, licking up any crumbs that fell, any tiny morsel that dropped from little hands.

"Sir," I said, "even the dogs eat the crumbs that fall from their master's table."

The room went quiet and Jesus looked at me long, a smile lifting the corner of his mouth. "What an answer!" he said. "I think it may be that you know something of my Father and live something of his ways." He paused looking at me keenly. "Tell me of your daughter."

I told him briefly of that awful night, and how my daughter had been since: her trances, her cries, her twisted laughter, her fear, and her perverse words. He watched me attentively, and I noticed the softening of compassionate love on his face as he listened. Finally I stopped and he spoke slowly. "Your faith has healed her," he said. "The demon is gone now. Go in peace, daughter. And may the God of all the nations go with you."

I jumped up, ready to leave immediately, but they persuaded me to stay. "You will not reach Tyre before midnight, anyway," they said. So I stayed the night, falling asleep quickly with the exhaustion of the day. I woke at first light with the usual heaviness over my heart, but, as I remembered, I felt a great excitement. I jumped up, wrapped a few morsels of food to eat on the way, and set out. As I walked, I tried to tell myself not to hope too much, but I knew everything had changed. When I burst into our room late that morning, she was still lying on the bed, but she had a little smile on her face as she listened to her sister telling her a story. Her eyes lit up as she saw me. "Mummy," she said, "I'm back now, and it's light again."

Mary's Reflection

She looked at me as she ended the story.

"She's a woman grown now," she said. "She has a child of her own, and a fine mother she is to her. Both my daughters are lovely mothers. They don't really understand what it cost me to make a home for them here. And I wouldn't tell them that. But that conversation with Jesus was a turning point in my life. Not just because he healed my daughter—that meant everything to me—but because something passed between us that day. The way he heard and named my knowing of the Father. It was true, and I knew it was true. I saw it in him, too: he knew the Father and recognized those who knew him."

"I always listened out for stories of him, you know. I heard about his mock trial and his death. I could hardly bear to imagine that man who had such a depth of God in him, crucified, nails tearing his body. But I *could* imagine his absolutely unswerving hold on truth, and on God."

We both wept as we remembered the man we loved, she so briefly yet clearly. "It is an evil world," she said. "But joy comes with the morning."

6

A Fractured Life Becomes a Cascade of Diamonds

The Widow of Nain[1]

LET ME TELL YOU another story of another mother whose child was restored to her. I remember the day it happened. After visiting villages near Galilee, we set out for Nain. It was hot and dusty and I just wanted us to finally get to a village where we could stop and find some shade and a cool drink. The men were discussing some theological detail, as they often did, trying to prove they understood something profound. I can't remember what it was; I only remember being hot and short-tempered and critical and wanting to walk a bit apart. At last I could see Nain in the distance—soon, some relief from the heat and the talk.

As we got closer, we could see a crowd coming through the town gates. It soon became evident that it was a funeral. We could hear the wailing. Part of me sympathized with the family, whoever they were, but part of me, too, was annoyed. We would have to wait for the crowd to come pushing through the gates before we

1. Luke 7:11–15.

54

could get in. We drew over, off the path to let them pass. The usual professional mourners were wailing, but I didn't bother to look at them closely. At the center of the procession beside the body, I saw a woman who was obviously distraught with grief. Her keening was that of a woman totally bereft, her grieving was indescribable, even to the eyes of a stranger. I looked away, unable to bear the pain in her face and the cries of utter despair. I pulled away from the mourners with the others. Except for Jesus—he stepped out into the path. He was never one to shrink from pain. He asked whose the body was. The woman herself could not speak for the cries that wracked her, but others were quick to tell the story.

This was a young, unmarried man, the only son of his widowed mother. They told the story as she stood weeping, her body bowed as if she carried a great weight under which she was hardly able to stand. Jesus turned to her and gently, with compassion in all of his being, told her not to weep. She looked at him, her eyes wide with tears and her face totally uncomprehending. I looked at her face: it was as though her whole world had collapsed to a never-ending weeping, a black, overwhelming agony.

Jesus' eyes did not leave her face. Her anguish seemed only to draw him closer. "Woman," he spoke again, "Do not weep. Your son will live." She still stared, uncomprehending. Sobs shook her small frame. Jesus touched her arm gently, and then turned to the body. "Young man," he said, "I say to you, get up."

Because I was watching only his face—that intentness with which he speaks healing into someone's life—I did not see what happened next. I was held by his passion to bring life, as if, in that moment, the rest of the world drops away from him and all of his being focuses into gift. I did not see, but I heard the collective gasp of the crowd. The woman's keening cut off, mid-breath. Then I saw Jesus reach down to the bier, and with others crowding around, he helped the young man to stand before his mother. Her face was utterly transformed. The tears and dust were still smeared across her face, but truly it was as though her face shone. She stared into her living son's eyes.

Jesus turned and looked at me with such utter, deep joy. All the voices had started again—a great babble of voices—but that intent delight lingered in him, and my own heart sang in response.

When I went back those years later to find her, to hear the story from her side, she described that moment as a rebirth. All of life looked different from that moment when her swirling, hopeless chaos turned into a dance of ecstasy. After we talked, I wrote something of her story, but it was her images that stayed with me. She spoke of fractured shards, of her body, dismembered inside. It was all darkness, as though the sun had been shrouded, until Jesus' touch had turned her life into diamonds.

All life is broken
    ended
        meaningless.
Everything jars
    and breaks apart.
My heart is torn
    out of me.
Shredded
    dismembered.
My being is fractured
    and I am undone.
And then:
Do not weep, he says.
It is as though he speaks another language
    for all the meaning it makes.
My soul has become a weeping
    and there is nothing else.
He turns towards the bier,
    and I cross the divide into eternity.
My son lives—and light cascades into brilliance
    dancing before me.
It is never far from me
    that cascading brilliance.
I see my son, now a father himself,
    living ordinary, everyday life.

But whenever I look at him
    I see that eternal light breaking in
        and touching all with diamonds.

7

Touching the Untouchable

The Woman Bleeding[1]

THAT JESUS COULD RAISE people from the dead was utterly amazing to us. Yes, Elijah had done that, but it was rare, even amongst our greatest prophets. We were in awe. I hadn't begun to travel consistently with Jesus; I hadn't been healed long myself. I wanted to be near him as much as I could. On the day that Jesus raised the little girl, Jairus' daughter, there was another healing before we ever got to Jairus' house. It started as an unwelcome interruption and delayed our response to Jairus' urgent summons.

Jesus stopped, dead still, and asked, "Who touched me?" There was such a crowd that day jostling about him. Jairus was a well-known leader in the synagogue and everyone had heard how sick his daughter was and wanted to be there to see what would happen. In the midst of this crowd, Jesus stopped and insisted on knowing who had touched him.

Funny, I had noticed the woman a few minutes earlier. She looked different from others in the excited, curious crowd. Her

1. Luke 8:41–48.

58

shawl was drawn about her face. The glimpse I had of her made me think she was a little strange. Her face was pale and drawn, with a furtive yet determined look. I had wondered what she was up to. When she finally came forward, at Jesus' insistence, she threw herself trembling at his feet. I was right beside him and I saw the look that passed between them. I realized the furtiveness had been fear, but as she met his eyes there was something close to exhilaration. As her story tumbled out, fear drained away and joy turned her face to radiance.

When I thought of searching for her, I remembered that look on her face. It must have been something similar to the look on my face in the moment of my own healing.

The Bleeding Woman's Story

What can I tell you of the first day I met Jesus? Do I remember it? Ah, my dear, of course I do. I see my life in three scenes: the birth of my child was the end of my first innocence, the end of life, as I had known it. The second part was a living death, a descent into hell. Meeting Jesus was the beginning of the restoration, the start of the third scene.

I grew up in Capernaum, here, on the shores of Galilee. I was happy enough as a child, just like all the other children, maybe a little on the quiet side. We would spend our days working and playing, helping in our home, getting food from the markets, sometimes going down to the lake to get fish as the fishing boats came in. Sometimes we would help in the fields nearby when the men were harvesting. Mine was as carefree as a child's life can be, I guess, with friendships here, little quarrels there, gossip and storytelling throughout. As often as we could, we took the days-long trek down to Jerusalem for the Passover. I especially enjoyed those days, the whole company of us traveling together, hearing the stories over again, singing the psalms as we walked, noticing the wayside flowers, and joining more families as we neared the city. I can't say I liked the press of crowds, the noise and dust. But I liked the evenings when we'd sit around together and hear the happenings of the year gone by—the babies born, the death of an old one, the marriage of the friend of a cousin. So the conversations went and I would listen and piece together the family relationships—who was related to whom and how far back the ties went.

We girls were allowed to go to the temple with the women to hear the priests chanting and feel the holiness of that sacred place. It used to give me goosebumps, the sacredness of it all: the laws and sacrifices and purifications. And then, the long journey back home. We slept under the stars as we traveled, said goodbyes along the way, made promises of reconnection. The older girls would talk of who they might marry and we all talked about having families and about childbirth. Sometimes, we whispered stories of rape and death. In those days, I saw life as mostly hopeful. I began to have dreams of my own life as a married woman with my own children and household to manage. We were comfortably well off and I expected I might marry someone with enough worldly goods to give me a peaceful life. As I said, that was a time of innocence, of knowing very little of the cruelty of life—the cruelty of people.

I remember, especially, the journey down to Jerusalem when I was twelve. One of my older friends, Hannah, had recently married and she and her husband were traveling with us. Two other friends were betrothed. All the talk was of weddings and babies, love and marriage—and what men were like. I said little, but of course I listened and daydreamed and stored up details for later wonderings. I remember the trip as being filled with songs and laughter—I'm not sure that it was very different from other times really. Perhaps it stands out because of the contrast to the journey back.

The first couple of days were the same as usual: buying food, meeting up with family and old friends, visiting the markets and the temple. And then, on one of the evenings we were all sitting around sharing stories of the year gone by, someone asked about a young cousin who had been recently married the last time we had been together. I remember the silence that followed the question. Then came the story of how she had died in childbirth. A long slow dying because the baby wouldn't come. It was too big, they thought, or maybe around the wrong way. I can't remember those details. But I will never forget the look on Hannah's face as I glanced around the room. She was white; the life was gone from her face and in its place, a look of horror, even terror. It was probably the first time I had realized the real possibility that one of us could die in childbirth. I saw my friend realize it too. I remember that evening so well. Not because of Hannah who, by the way, went on to have five healthy children of her own with nothing more than the usual pain and morning sickness.

No, I remember it because I came to envy that young woman who died. Awful as it may sound, I came to envy her in the years ahead. I sank so low that a long, agonizing death seemed preferable to the living death that my life became.

Our journey back from Jerusalem was much more sober. Somehow the stories of death and illness and poverty seemed to have multiplied. The Roman occupation seemed even more harsh; it was an inkling of things to come. Still, I was little more than a child. As we reached Galilee, feelings of comfort and safety returned. The gladness of being received into the security of home and community came over me once more. The next year, when I started menstruating, I remember my first feeling was one of joining the women of the world, the mothers, the child-bearers. Even though some of the shame and uncleanness were there, I remember it best as a feeling of hope and belonging.

My parents eventually found a husband for me, and I too went through the excitement of betrothal and preparation for marriage. My friends were having children and the story we had heard in Jerusalem faded into the background. I remember that time as an extension of the innocence. It lasted even into marriage to a man I had known only a little. I remember my shyness and inexperience of our early marriage. I began to know his world and find my place in the extended family. I took a while to get pregnant but I wasn't worried. I was young and there was a lot of learning to do. I'd visit friends and hold their babies and learn as much as I could. Two of my brothers had married, so I visited my sisters-in-law and helped with their children a little.

My mother-in-law accepted me into the family, of course, but she was demanding in her own way. She kept to the laws and regulations, the purity codes. She knew more about my personal life than I wanted her to know and made sure I observed the rules around menstruation and uncleanness. I knew the usual customs of being unclean for seven days each month, but she was especially strict. She was trying to teach me, I'm sure, quoting me the Levitical lines, "Whoever touches her is unclean and everything upon which she sits is unclean."

I remember being so excited when I got pregnant, noticing the changes in my body, and watching my husband's face lose its usual reserve to satisfaction and contentment. Ours would not be the first grandchild on either side, so there was less excitement in the extended families, but that let me keep to myself a little and savor the new life growing inside me. I talked to the baby all the time and I remember so well when I felt the first kicks and movement in my growing belly. Such a time of hope, those weeks before it all came crashing down.

I'd been helping out at the wedding of my husband's cousin. We carried the food back and forth and helped clean afterward. I remember being particularly tired. It wasn't a lot more work than usual, so I don't think it was anything I'd done. Of course, I went over this a hundred times in the weeks that followed. I started having labor pains that night, though I did not think of them as that. I wondered if I'd eaten something bad at the wedding, but eventually it got worse and worse. I didn't want to believe it was premature labor, but finally my husband fetched his mother and she took charge.

My little child was born. There was blood everywhere—I couldn't stop bleeding. I went in and out of consciousness and the only memory I have of it is like a nightmare where people come and go, changing images and pain. I never even held my baby. I lost everything in one endless night. Apparently, the bleeding eventually slowed, but I was so weak by then, I could do nothing but sleep and wake and accept spoonfuls of soups and nasty-tasting potions. My mother-in-law tried to keep me separate from the family. She seemed to have gathered a bunch of old women to come in and out and care for me. Of course, death is part of life and miscarriages are not uncommon. But I had lost so much blood that I was very anemic. It took weeks to recover my strength. During that time I hardly saw my husband. There were always other women around.

Worst, the bleeding didn't stop. Sometimes, it would slow and I would think that at last it was over and I would recover. But nothing seemed to help. My mother-in-law and her cronies seemed to discover all sorts of possible remedies. Always, I carried the sense of shame, of uncleanness, of becoming an untouchable.

No one ever spoke of my child, my little companion through those hopeful pregnant months. To them it had not been a child. But for me it was my future, my future motherhood, and the baby, a real little being with whom I had a relationship already. No one seemed to want to talk about that, but acted as though we should all focus on life—and other chances later. I cried in secret and tried to surrender my baby to the God of the heavens who gives life and takes it away. I let go my dreams one by one and tried to focus on getting better.

After weeks, months it must have been, I persuaded my parents to take me home. I thought being with them might help me. My mother-in-law agreed to relinquish some control. She was probably getting worn out with it all, herself. In those early days we were still hopeful. My father even arranged for physicians to come. I had to submit to their questions and examinations, but nothing helped. They gave their various opinions and diagnoses. Slowly, they began to include future predictions—having another child was not one of them.

So there I was, eighteen months previously I had been pregnant with all of life before me. Now, I found myself weak and childless and dependent on my parents. At first my husband would send messages asking after my health, but over time these lessened. I faced the possibility of losing him as well. Who would want a wife who was continuously ritually unclean? I could not have a marriage relationship, could not have children. No one would blame him for ending the marriage.

A year became two and still, the bleeding. There is an old saying that the life is in the blood. As I bled week after week, month after month, year in and year out, I felt as though my life was ebbing away. My strength and purpose diminished, my life closed in. I seldom left the house. I used what little energy I had to help around the house as much as I could, to make at least some contribution. The sense of uncleanness always came heavily on me when I went out. I would hear my mother-in-law's voice: "Whoever touches her is unclean." I would hurry through the streets so as not to touch anyone; I averted my eyes so not to be recognized.

Now and then we would hear of yet another remedy or healer, and a contrary hope would spring up: maybe this one, maybe this time. Maybe I could begin my life again, maybe I could return to my husband, maybe I could have a child after all. And I would try the next remedy, another concoction of herbs. I would try to ignore the rumors of healing because I was tired of the disappointments and worn out with the fruitless searching.

Another year went by. My mother became ill and died and my father, too, was getting on in years. I tried to help as best I could. We shared what little comfort we had, but it was a bleak time. And then I received the bill of divorce. It was honorable that my husband had held out as long as he had. But he wanted to get on with his life; he needed a family and a companion. It plunged me into despair. Those were black years. It was then that I would remember the young woman who died in childbirth those years ago. I wished that my life had ended back there, back in Jerusalem when all of life seemed hopeful. I would even welcome a slow, agonizing death in place of this slow, agonizing life in which there was no life. I saw no point in living and had no one to care if I lived or died.

My father thoughtfully left something for me when he died. Though I lived with one of my brothers, at least I wasn't to be totally dependent on them. At thirty, I felt like an old woman, a recluse, an untouchable. And still I would find myself trying another new remedy, another physician, another charlatan. My inheritance dwindled, spent on so-called remedies that, in fact, only made me worse.

Through all of this I would cry out to God. I would quote the psalms, "O Lord, why dost thou cast me off? Why dost thou hide thy face from me? Afflicted and close to death from my youth up, I suffer thy terrors, I am helpless. Thy wrath has swept over me; thy dread assaults destroy me. Thou hast caused lover and friend to shun me."[2] I was comforted that others must have known the torment and despair that I did. As time went on—ten, eleven, twelve years—I began to question what this God of ours was like. My favorite psalms were the songs of desolation. I was comforted not to feel so alone. I began to notice that after the psalmist laid out his complaint to God, he would claim that God was worthy of praise. He seemed to believe his prayer effective. "Turn again, O God of hosts! Look down from heaven and see."[3] "In distress you called and I delivered you."[4] "Incline thy ear, O Lord, and answer me, for I am poor and needy . . . But thou, O Lord, art a God merciful and gracious."[5]

As I cried out to God, I began to tell him just what it was like for me—how poor and needy and untouchable I felt. And sometimes I would remind him that he was merciful and gracious. Slowly, I found myself to be in a different place. There were the tiniest shoots of hope again. But they were different. I no longer expected marriage and children. I even began to imagine I could live some kind of life with this chronic bleeding. I began to trust that the God of the heavens could somehow still be gracious to me. My life was not over. Somehow, my life might be fruitful. Some days I noticed a pain in my chest—daring to hope was painful. I had extinguished hope because the pain had seemed too much to bear. So I began to speak aloud my hope in God, the one who does not forget us, the one who lifts up the downtrodden.

I heard of another healer. One who cared for children and for lepers. He had made the lame walk and the blind see. Surely he was worth trying. But I heard that everywhere he went crowds

2. Ps 88:14–16, 18.
3. Ps 80:14.
4. Ps 81:7.
5. Ps 86:1,15.

followed him. The thought filled me with horror. I would have to push through crowds of people. Untouchable that I was, I could not bring uncleanness to others. As I imagined myself in the crowd, another horror hit me, and I was filled with shame. He would know! If I went to him and asked for healing, everyone would know the uncleanness I had spread. If I just came begging for healing, saying nothing of my condition, he would look and see and know what I had done and who I was. He would know that in laying hands on me to give me healing, he had become unclean himself. I put the possibility away. I couldn't do it.

But the idea persisted. Why would I put off this opportunity when it might bring the healing I had hoped for, asked God for? I couldn't keep praying and not do what I could do. I imagined it again: pushing through the crowds. Maybe I could just reach out and touch him through the crowd. Surely that would be enough to heal me—just to touch him? He didn't have to know anything. I hated the thought of making him unclean, ashamed that my touch could do that—especially to someone who would know.

Well, what about his garment then? What about just the hem of his robe, the tassel on the corner? Now that struck me as funny. The law said that the cord of blue in the tassel was to remind us to follow the commands of the Lord instead of our own ways.[6] This persistence was beginning to feel like the command of God.

I would go then. I would hide myself in the crowd with my shawl around my face and I would find a way to touch the tassel, the corner of his robe. As I planned, I felt as though I was making an agreement with God. I'll go and do this, but you'll make sure no one knows. I wasn't sure that God was agreeing to this plan, but I was determined to do what I could and leave the future in God's hands.

It took three tries. I went out one day, but the crowd was just too big. I went another time only to find he had gone with his disciples across to the other side of the lake. It was then that I realized how determined I was to do this. My disappointment and frustration sent me home in tears. When I heard he was back, I hurried

6. Num15:38.

out. I listened carefully to the talk of the gathering crowd. "Jairus' daughter is dying," they said. "He's asked Jesus to go to his house." Ah, I knew where that was, near the synagogue where Jairus was a leader. I knew some short cuts through alleyways. Maybe I could catch up with him. This time, *this* time. I hurried, my head down, my shawl pulled around my face. I could feel my heart beating as I hurried through the streets, the little energy I had slipping away. I could hear the crowd ahead and I prayed to the God of my hope that I would reach him. As I came down an alleyway near the synagogue, I saw people ahead. Head down, I pushed my way through. "Yes, that must be him. There is Jairus hurrying beside him, talking to him about his daughter," I thought. Then, right ahead of me, was the blue cord in the tassel of the garment. Jesus paused to hear what Jairus was saying and I reached out through the people around him. "Oh, heal me now, God of mercy," I prayed, and touched it with my fingertips. It was the merest brush of my fingertips, but in that instant I felt a flood of energy I hadn't felt in years. I stopped dead still, letting the crowd push past me. In my focus, I had put aside my uncleanness for a moment, but now I felt the familiar shame flood back as people jostled up against me in the crowd. But what was this? The crowd had stopped and the chatter quieted.

I heard a voice of quiet authority saying, "Who was it that touched me?" I bent my head and pulled my shawl more tightly about my face. Anyone who recognized me would know the shameful thing I had done. How could he know? He couldn't know. I only touched the corner of his robe. When no one answered, I heard one of the men say, "Master, the multitudes surround you and press upon you!" "Yes," I thought, "lots of people touched him. And God, I did what I told you I would—I didn't really touch him!" I heard Jairus urging him to hurry. But he persisted "No, someone touched me. I felt the power go from me."

I can't describe the rush of thoughts that tumbled through my head: "He's never going to get to Jairus' little girl. Oh, the shame of this crowd knowing what I have done. He knows! He knows it's me. I'm healed and all the world should know what God has done. Oh what will they think of me when they know?" But then,

I knew I couldn't hide. I looked up and saw him looking at me. In his eyes was a look I could not fathom. I stepped towards him, the crowds pulling back to give me room, Jairus waiting impatiently at his elbow. I fell to the ground. He bent to hear me and in tears I told him the truth—in front of all those people. "For twelve years I have been bleeding. Nothing could heal me. I have lost my child, my husband. I have paid everything I had to try and get well. I touched the edge of your shawl. And oh, sir, I know I am healed!"

He reached out and lifted me up. I kept my eyes on his face as he pulled back my shawl. He looked at me deeply and said, "Daughter, your faith has made you well; go in peace." I stood there in front of all those people, my shawl back from my face, out in public for the first time in twelve years. He put his hand under my elbow and gently turned me to face them. He said it again: "Your faith has made you well."

As I walked back through the streets, I held my head high. I realized what he had done. He had honored me in front of all those people. He had healed me from my shame by speaking of my faith. He had touched me and so had openly broken the purity codes. He had healed me physically and emotionally, socially and intellectually. And then I remembered: "But God, what about our agreement? This was going to be a secret!" And if I'd ever heard God speak, I did then: "What agreement? That was your agreement. My agreement was that you would do what you could and I would do what I could." And it felt as though the God of the heavens laughed a great laugh that welled up in my heart and spilled over in tears. I hurried through the streets, my face shining with tears and laughter for anyone to see.

I never did get married again; I never had children. Somehow, I didn't want that dream anymore. Instead, I became a midwife. I sat with people through their labor. I felt the utter joy of seeing children arrive into this life. And sometimes I helped when there was a miscarriage or a stillbirth. I seem to have the knack for saying the right words at the right time or just sitting in silence in the grief and the pain. And I tell them, I always tell them, how loved they are of God. I tell them of the God who is also a nursing mother and a midwife, a woman in labor and a shepherd who cares for those who are with young. And, I do not believe any more that this God sees us as unclean. Jesus showed me that God has broken the purity codes once and for all. The mothers are most to be honored, and the ones who miscarry to be cared for with special attentiveness.

Mary's Reflection

She saw my own tears as I listened to her story and her old knuckled hand stroked mine. "Ah, my dear, you too know the pain of loss, don't you? May Mother God hold you and give you peace."

8

A Soldier Recognizes Authority

The Roman Centurion[1]

ALTHOUGH OUR COUNTRY WAS under the oppression of the Romans, we tried as much as possible to live our lives ignoring their presence. Jesus seldom spoke of them, living out the truth that he was called to the lost sheep of the house of Israel. Nevertheless, we would encounter a soldier occasionally, or even interact with one. The most memorable interaction was with the Roman centurion who lived in Capernaum, the same town as Jairus. In fact, this man built the synagogue for the people and had clearly shown reverence for our God. When he sent elders of the Jews to ask Jesus to heal his servant, I saw Jesus respond to the need as he would any other request: he went with them to lay hands on the paralyzed man. Others came, reporting that the centurion had said he was not worthy. I was astonished at his humility. Jesus, too, had marveled at his faith. I did not meet him then, but when I was in

1. Luke 7:2–10.

Capernaum gathering stories from others, I remembered his story. My curiosity was piqued.

I was a little afraid that he would not be willing to have me in his house, but he was a most unusual man. He clearly loved our people. He invited me in with grace and respect.

The Roman Centurion's Story

A Roman centurion makes an unlikely believer, you'd think. And back at the beginning, I wasn't really a believer—not a true convert. I lived a rather compromised lifestyle. I certainly needed the goodwill of the Jewish authorities, but it was more than that. My mother had been a religious woman, always making a sacrifice to some god or observing some ritual. My father was away a lot—he was a Roman soldier, too, and very proud of it. During much of my childhood, he was away fighting some battle for supremacy. Then he'd be back boasting of courageous deeds, another rebellion put down, revolutionaries killed. Sometimes he'd start to describe the details and my mother would stop him with a look at me and my sister. My father would stop then, if my sister were there. He had a soft spot for her, but if she wasn't around, he'd keep talking. "The boy needs toughening up," he would say, and tell some gruesome story that would give me nightmares.

The next day, my mother would find a way to take me to the temple, offer some sacrifice, and tell me the gods would protect me. Even when I was really quite young, her religious superstitions would make me uncomfortable. I felt as though we were part of this endless haggling with the gods for safety. She'd get sick a lot and would often be trying some new cure or sacrificing to a new god. Even with all that, there was something in me that was drawn, too. My father's brash, egotistical concreteness didn't sit well with me. His "kill or be killed and that's the end of it" was far too superficial.

I was immersed in their religious tug-of-war—not just their beliefs, but the way each of them was. My father tried to fit me for a world of soldiers and my mother tried to keep her family safe.

71

Underneath all of it, something in me felt different from my dog-eat-dog father who believed that only might is right. I even felt different from the other boys I played with. Sometimes when my mother had me at some ritual, I'd pray my own prayer to the gods. I was searching for something deeper than the haggling and bargaining. I sensed it in a thunderstorm or under the stars at night or with the first buds of spring. Something of the beauty in a sunset or the sun sparkling on the water reached me. I sensed that the first birdcall at dawn or even the artisans with the beauty of their craft at their finger-tips were somehow sacred.

My mother died before I was a teenager, so of course my father got his way: I had to train to be a soldier. It was never a good fit. I took many blows and, later, sword wounds, but slowly, I got the hang of some of the moves. My love of beauty helped me in the end, because I loved a well-honed skill. I wanted the thrust and parry of combat properly executed. So I'd practice and practice. Needless to say, this pleased some of the trainers who gave me enough time to build up some skills and learn to hold my own.

That's when I first took an interest in training and supervising. I'd watch the trainers who got the best out of us recruits. It wasn't the ones who lorded it over us, ridiculing or provoking. It was the one or two who cared for us, not in a soft way, but in the way they called out our best and expected obedience, hard work, and long practice. There was one I watched in particular. He was quiet yet exacting; he called for absolute discipline but was totally just. He let us know he wanted our best. He related to all of us trainees with a complete authority, and he got what he commanded. It was from him that I first started seeing a way you could manage men without resorting to violence or being the toughest. I had the slightest hope that I could possibly survive in the Roman army, then. Perhaps, I could even hold some kind of rank. I watched and learned to respect and choose the best for others. I treated others well, both in and out of training. And gradually I began to get respect, too.

There was the other side of life for us teenage boys, also. Discovering sex, finding the street women, experimenting on our own. And, again, I knew I was different. There was a whole different undertone for me. Of course, I tried not to show too much. Life was hell if you were too different. For me there were longings for tenderness and hopeless crushes on other boys. I realized that women just didn't turn me on. There was enough male-to-male sex that I still hoped I was just going through some stage. Maybe I was stuck in some variation that everyone tries sometimes. But the hidden side of me seemed to grow deeper and stronger: my love of beauty, overwhelming tenderness, heart-lurching longing. I cried out to the gods for their intervention.

Eventually, the God of gods answered me—that's all I can put it down to. I was posted here to Palestine, this little god-forsaken, dusty corner of the empire where rebellion seems to be innate to the people. And I found it not so god-forsaken after all. I began to see why rebellion was intrinsic.

I'd learned my lessons of authority and management, and, along the way, I had become a centurion—a good one, too. My men respected me and I respected them. Even those who grudgingly obeyed only the power of the empire at my back usually began to see that I always chose to act justly.

The spiritual hunger of my boyhood stayed with me. Wherever I went I found excuse to visit a temple or examine the religious beliefs of the people. Always, the results were the same: disappointment and dissatisfaction in the bargaining games of the capricious, untrustworthy, fickle gods. None seemed much different than those who had taken my mother in spite of all her rituals and pleading.

The God of the Hebrews was different, though. At first I didn't realize it. There were endless sacrifices, holy days, and rituals. But slowly I heard enough about their God to make me really listen. This was a God who was one, not many. This God cared for the oppressed and stood for justice—and for mercy. The Hebrew God called his people to look at the beauty of creation and to care for their land. This God's laws were different, too: leave the land lying fallow, take a day of Sabbath rest, leave corners of the fields for the poor, and observe a day of atonement for repentance and expectation of God's grace. I was struck by the stories of patently imperfect men and women who were honored by their God because their hearts were for him. Prophets through the centuries called this God's people back to mercy, humility, and purity. In spite of all the sacrifices I saw, God actually said he wanted obedience and a humble heart rather than sacrifice. Above all of this, God, steadfast in his love, interacted with his people.

What I had initially understood to be rebellion was actually about this God. These people were willing to die rather than lose their God. They had suffered slavery in Egypt without being absorbed into that culture because they refused to give up the worship of *this* God. Exiled and oppressed by other nations before our own time, they clung tenaciously to their faith in *this* God. Gradually, I came to love this stubborn people and to love their responsive, interventionist God, so when I was moved to Capernaum, I had a synagogue built for them. I got to know the local leaders and conversed with their priests. I kept a check on my soldiers who developed some level of respect between themselves and the local community. All in all those were good years.

But there was a side to my life that these Jews didn't care for. My teenage preference for men rather than women had never changed. I had been discrete when I learned that the Jewish scriptures considered such practices abominable to their God. I did not know how to make sense of this. If their God was indeed the Creator God I had come to admire, even worship, had he not created me thus? I knew not; I could only respect the local people and their traditions. So my servant whom I loved and kept as my own, was ever only a servant to any visitors. Who knew how much they guessed or turned a blind eye to? I would wonder sometimes if they only respected me because I had power, because I gave them their place of worship. I could not ever really know what went on below the surface, but the peace held and our interactions were smooth.

I always kept an ear to the religious talk, curious to hear of any named as prophets or teachers. That's how I heard about Jesus. There was talk of him healing people and doing miracles, but what piqued my curiosity was the reported way he spoke about their

God. He called him Abba, father, and spoke as if they were on intimate terms. They said he spoke about money and business and relationships. He taught about caring for each other and relating to a God who was both just and merciful. It sounded to me as though he was a man who had tried to understand, as I had, what enabled men to live in respect, what enabled society to function, what enabled communities to truly care for all.

Coming in to the back of a crowd and catching some of his words, I managed to hear Jesus a couple of times. What struck me from the first was his authority. He spoke with truth and fearlessness, as if, I thought that first time, he had all the power of Rome to back him up. Even when he challenged some of the religious leaders about their legalistic demands, he spoke as if he had a source of authority greater than theirs. I went home pondering. Where had he learned that authority in this land oppressed and fragmented by political and religious factions since his birth? It was when I saw him healing people that I knew. He spoke without arrogance, without placing himself in a position of power, yet with such authority. To those he healed he said with respect, "Your faith has made you well." Yet, at the same time, he held a steady expectation that what he said would be done.

The only way I could understand was to compare it with what I had learned as a teenager by watching the masters at work. Those who knew that what they did was just, that what they required was what Rome required, spoke with that same expectation of obedience, knowing the empire was behind them. This Jesus held that same stance. His words about his God revealed his understanding of how God and authority interacted. He could command something and it would be done, because being under God's authority gave him authority. He could command and expect even the spirits to obey. I pondered this. If I was right, this man was a representative of the God of the heavens and the earth.

I was fascinated by all of this, but it remained somewhat hypothetical until my servant got sick. This was my servant whom I loved, the lover I tried to keep secret so as not to offend my Jewish friends. I tried the usual remedies. Nothing helped. I paid for expensive doctors. He only got worse. I could not bear to lose him, this man who had become so close to me.

I humbled myself and went to my Jewish friends. How could I go to Jesus? I was a Roman centurion, a foreigner. In his eyes, I was surely a sinner. I went to the elders in the synagogue and requested that they go and ask him for healing. They saw my anguish and promised they would do all they could. The servants who accompanied them returned with the news that Jesus was coming.

What? This was not what I had asked for. They told me what the elders had said to Jesus. "He is worthy to have you do this for him, for he loves our nation, and he built us our synagogue," they had told him. No! This was not the way I had meant. As if I deserved his presence. As if—why, it reminded me of the haggling my mother used to do with the Roman gods. "This Roman centurion does so much—he deserves to get what he wants." But it had nothing to do with deserving. It was about coming to the God of gods in humility with the recognition that if we line up with his ways, we can ask for his touch because of who he is. It had nothing to do with deserving. I wasn't worthy for him to even come to me.

What was I to do? I knew that he could merely speak the word and it would be done. I could only tell him that I recognized that I also held authority and was under authority. This time I went to one of the men I considered a friend, and I begged him: "Please go and meet Jesus. Please say to him only what I ask you to say. Please speak to him with all the respect of one who knows the God of gods. Say this to him: 'Lord, do not trouble yourself for I am not worthy to have you come under my roof; therefore I did not presume to come to you. But say the word and let my servant be healed. For I am a man set under authority, with soldiers under me: and I say to one, "Go" and he goes, and to another, "Come" and he comes, and to my slave, "Do this" and he does it.' Please go and say this to Jesus and he will understand."

He left, promising me he would say only this. I went back to the bedside of my lover. He lay paralyzed and obviously close to the end, unless the mercy of a merciful God intervened. I tried to count how long it would take, where my servants had said Jesus was, where he would have got to now. It was impossible to calculate with the crowds who trailed him and forever pleaded his attention. I prayed. I begged the God of the Jews to hear me, even as I told him I was sorry for begging. I no longer believed in a God who needed bargaining and begging, but I knew not what else to do. I sat with tears running down my cheeks as I watched my lover hardly breathing. I was silent and still for what seemed like hours.

And then, he moved under my hand. I opened my eyes to see him open his. "Why are you crying?" he asked me. And in that moment I knew what the true God was like. I answered, "Because God is a father to the fatherless, a healer of the undeserving. He speaks and it is done."

When my friend returned from meeting Jesus, he told me what had happened. He had said to Jesus what I had asked him to say. Jesus had marveled and turned to the crowd and said, "I tell you, not even in Israel have I found such faith."

I count myself a real believer from that day. On that day, I knew that God was who I had come to understand him to be: a God who gives to all men liberally, pours out his mercy on any who turn to him, and blesses humans with the authority and responsibility to touch the lives of others.

Mary's Reflection

My heart had warmed to this man as I listened to him speak. It was clear that he loved the God of Abraham, Isaac, and Jacob. It was obvious that he lived a most unusual life, compromised by his love of God and our people. Yet he managed to continue in his duties and keep peace in the neighborhood through his good relationships. Knowing he could be recalled and sent elsewhere at any time, he had developed a trust in God that allowed him to live day by day at peace with himself and with others. He treated me with respect and kindness and, as I left, reminded me I was a sister in the faith in a growing community of believers.

9

Darkness, Light, and Seeing Both

The Man Born Blind[1]

I WASN'T THERE ON the day that Jesus healed the man born blind. None of us were there at the actual healing, because Jesus sent him to wash off the mud he put on his eyes in the pool of Siloam. It was yet another occasion of Jesus healing on the Sabbath, and we didn't understand the repercussions until afterwards. Over time, I met all of the man's family, and it was this story that demonstrated to me that Jesus was not only touching individual lives. The ripples of each healing, each transformation, washed across other lives and invited each to respond to the mystery of a God who stoops into our everyday reality.

1. John 9:1–41.

The Blind Man's Story

My life is divided in two. The first half dark, the second half light. It was not dark for me then—only now, looking back, I know it as dark. Then it was felt and heard, now it is seen. Then I was dependent, now I look after myself and care for others. Then I was an outsider, I was invisible. Well, that's how people treated me. I was visible only in the moment they threw a coin or two into my cup. But even then they often kept talking to each other as though I wasn't there. I wasn't really a person when I was blind.

I listened to the talk as people walked by or stopped to tell the latest gossip in twos or threes. I knew what was going on as well as anyone. I knew more, probably, because I learned to listen beneath the words. I heard the hopes and fears, the politics, the God-talk, the stories, the prices, and the longing for liberation. Sometimes I would hear tell of someone healed of an illness, and of course I would listen for every clue: what they did, who the healer might be, what prayer they prayed, what sacrifices they made. I always hoped, despite my parents warning me from a young age: "But not you child." No one had ever heard of healing for one born blind.

Any talk of healing came with the God-talk: sin offerings, sacrifices, prayers to an Almighty God—who didn't seem so almighty, except maybe in olden times. I had asked once as a child what I had to do to be like the other children: how could I run off on my own, climb trees, help with work? This question obviously pained my mother deeply. "Hush child, you must accept the lot you have been given." Only later did I realize her anguish as I learned what they said our God was like. God punishes the evildoer and blesses the righteous. Obviously, since I could hardly have been an evildoer right back in her womb, God must have been punishing her with my blindness. I puzzled at that—my mother who prayed all the prayers, kept the Sabbath, ate only food she prepared according to the laws. I could not imagine what she had done. But the family's silence left only a sense of shame and unspoken guilt. And knowing myself as the cause of the shame, I did not speak of it either.

I wondered about this God of ours. It was very clear to me, as I listened to the stories around me, that the very unrighteous were sometimes blessed and the unholy were sometimes seen as the holy men. I used to listen to the scribes and the Pharisees talk, too. They were oblivious to me listening, but I knew they were simply men like the rest of us.

I was an outsider. Even on days when I most wished I could be healed and could contribute to the family's needs, I was secretly glad I was outside their systems and their hierarchies, outside all their keeping of rules. I did not have to bow my head to those in power just because they had power. Being on the outside let me see what those who were caught in the lines of power were blind to.

I heard talk of Jesus long before he ever came into my life. Rumors of healers and prophets were rife in our times of such oppression. I heard the talk of healing—even healing of blind men—and the old hope stirred within me. I knew better than to say anything. My parents' oft-repeated "But not you child," had silenced any words I might speak. But still I listened with my usual curiosity. He seemed to heal with simply a word, maybe a touch. Even lepers were cleansed. At first I doubted that one. Not real lepers, I thought. But more tales of that story reached my ears. He sent a whole group of them to the priest and on the way they were healed. I imagined it: setting off to find a priest, with no evidence of healing. I imagined them talking to each other. Maybe one said, "But not to us, no healing for us." Perhaps another reminded him of the story of Naaman dipping in the River Jordan, in faith that it would heal him.

I also heard of the controversy surrounding him. Some said he was a charlatan, a Nazarene. "What good came out of Nazareth?" as the saying went. I wondered what it would be like to be rejected because of where you were born? Or how you were born, I thought, and knew the answer to that one. I heard that he spoke of a new age, an age where the poor would have good news. How could that be? I was poor; my family was poor. What could happen to make any difference? If only the rich would share with us their riches. That could only mean changed hearts—could people really change like that?

I heard that Jesus was unimpressed with the religious rulers. He even spoke out against them and their pious ways. I agreed with him on that—but what good would it do him to challenge them? He spoke of God as a father, not just a righteous judge. Well, I would need to see more proof of that to believe.

I was an outsider. I was invisible. I heard the talk. I sat at my street corner collecting my meager offerings and I wondered. I could do nothing.

Then, the day came that divided my life in two. It started like all the others. It was a Sabbath day, but no different for me. Feeling my way to the corner, I set out my blanket and my cup. I listened to the whirl of talk: rumors of Jesus again. People were passing by. I heard an unknown, rough country voice, "Rabbi, who sinned, this man or his parents, that he was born blind?" I was invisible again. I turned away not even wanting to hear the answer. But I did hear it. "It was not that this man sinned or his parents."[2] The words were spoken with such authority that the shame I carried was suddenly all in question. I swung back, totally attentive. "But that the works of God might be made manifest in him, we must work the works of him who sent me, while it is day; night comes, when no one can work. As long as I am in the world, I am the light of the world."

I felt someone sit down beside me. Then his voice again, "You seem deep in thought." I nodded, "I'm listening to what you said." "And what do you think of what you heard?" he asked. I was startled. No one cared what I thought of what I heard. "I want to know what you meant. What did you mean about God's works being manifest?" I felt the intentness of his presence, felt myself seen as never before.

---

2. John 9:3. There are neither verses nor punctuation (except the question mark) in ancient Greek. I have taken the liberty of changing the placing of the full-stop at this point as does Hobbs. See Hobbs, Herschel H. *The Gospel of John*, Grand Rapids, MI: Baker Book House, 1972, p161. Hobbs notes that G.Campbell Morgan (1863–1945) a leading biblical scholar, makes the same translation, changing the meaning of Jesus' words to say the man's sight is God's purpose, not his blindness.

"And how is it that you would like to see God's works manifest? What is it that *you* want?" he asked me quietly, but with great attention. "Oh, to see of course," I said before I could even stop the words. There was a small silence and then I felt his hands on my eyes. I was seldom touched by a stranger, certainly not with such tenderness. He ran his palms and his fingers over my face, gently lifting my eyelids, speaking quiet words of prayer to his father God. And he asked me again, checking to see that I really understood, "If you could see, your life would be very different. You would become one of the providers." "That is what I long for," I told him. "Then I will send you to wash away the blindness," he told me. He explained that he would put clay on my eyes and that I must go to the pool of Siloam to wash it off. I felt the coolness of the clay as he placed it over my eyes, his hands again touching my face with tenderness.

I went, of course, feeling my way along the walls and thinking of Naaman, thinking of the lepers. I would go for only the tiniest chance of healing, but His words and his fingers had touched me much more deeply than anyone would have seen.

I doubt that anyone not born blind can imagine what it is like to suddenly emerge from a life of sound and touch to a visual world. Suddenly my narrow space opened into a myriad of colors and shapes. Objects close enough to touch I knew, but many shapes—houses, trees, people beyond my hearing of them—were strange. At first it was all too much. Color and shape collided and I knew little of what I saw, until I closed my eyes and the world came to rights again. I sat there by the pool in utter wonderment. I opened my eyes and tried to understand. Crying in gratitude and laughing in amazement, I shut my eyes again to get my bearings. I opened them for a glimpse of light and color. The sky above was blue. What a wonder. That was blue—they had told me about blue, but it had meant nothing. And now I saw such a clash of colors that I simply sat and stared.

During those first days, all the images blurred together. I did not know what it was meant to be like. I had to learn to focus and separate shape from shape, movement and distance and proportion. I didn't even know how to learn it. I only knew the amazing, miraculous mix of light and dark. I experienced the sudden recognition of something familiar as I felt its shape and then learned what it looked like. People's faces amazed me: the differences, the expressions, the profiles, the looks in their eyes. A face I didn't know would suddenly become known when the person spoke and I recognized a familiar voice. But I get ahead of myself—it took time to learn to interpret faces and streets and places by sight.

That first day I had to find the way home by closing my eyes and feeling my way. I came to the doorway of our home and listened to see who was present. My mother spoke to one of my sisters and I knew them by their voices. I went to my mother and told her I could see. "Oh, child, no!" she exclaimed, as she might have done when I was small. I could hear only fear and disbelief in her voice. "But yes, mother!" and I told her of my encounter with Jesus, of the clay on my eyes, and of the pool at Siloam. I shared the wonder of light and dark and the utter blueness of the sky. She listened and I could feel the unease of her silence. "But on the Sabbath?" she queried. "What will people say?" "But mother, he healed me! It could only be God. It has to be from God to make *me* see!"

It was not much better when my father came in. "You just don't know what dark powers he might have used," he said. Their doubt made no sense to me at all, and I tried to persuade them, "But we've never heard of this happening to anyone ever before—it *must* be God who has done this for me!"

One of my sisters was nearly as excited as I was. Because of her, the neighbors began to come in and see for themselves. People I recognized by their voices began to speak to me directly as though I had become a real, visible person to them. Over the days, I learned to focus. I matched faces to voices and I learned to recognize people by sight. There was much talk in our street then. People questioned how this miracle could be. Some even suggested I'd never been blind in the first place. Maybe I was only pretending to see, they guessed. But as soon as they came to see for themselves, they had to admit the truth.

Initially, I reveled in all the interest. I enjoyed being seen and spoken to like an adult. But, after a while, I began to tire of the questions, the disbelief, and especially the fear. People acted as if I had done something wrong to gain my sight. They hinted that I should have refused to be healed or waited for a day designated for that purpose. People would come and ask me again and again how it happened and then begin questioning me about Jesus. What else did he do? Where was he now?

Should I know everything about him? One of our neighbors, old Jethro, wanted to take me to the Pharisees for their verdict. I didn't see the point of it, but he was an old man and kind to me, so I agreed to go with him. A group of others tagged along, curious to hear what was said, but my parents hung back, afraid of the attention this was all bringing.

Old Jethro took me to the temple where I stood in awe of the columns and the height of the building and the decoration. It was Jethro who told the Pharisees my story: how I'd been born blind, been confined to begging all my life, and then been given my sight by this healer. So they turned to me and spoke to me. For the first time in my life a Pharisee asked for my opinion: "How did you get your sight?" Jethro had just told them the story, even mentioning it was on the Sabbath day, so I reiterated briefly, "He put clay on my eyes, then I washed, and now I see."

They began to argue with each other about the Sabbath—the same point my parents had raised. "He must be a sinner to break the Sabbath day by doing this work of healing." "But how could he be a sinner and do this miracle?" So it went on, this talk swirling around me as though I didn't exist, until finally one of them turned to me again, "What do you say about him, since he has opened your eyes?"

What could I say? It seemed obvious to me. Indeed my eyes had been opened. "Why, he is a prophet." That started the arguments again. Finally, one of them looked at me contemptuously—I was struck by the power a look could have—and said, "He probably wasn't born blind at all." What could I say? For a moment

I had been visible to them, I had been a real person; now they dismissed my story, dismissed my truth.

I turned and left, my brief encounter with the religious leaders confirming what I had secretly believed: they were just men like other men, caught by their position and rigid beliefs. They would not allow God to be outside their categories.

As I found my way back through the streets, some of my neighbors came hurrying up behind me, exclaiming, "They want to see your parents now." "Whatever for?" I asked, imagining my mother's anxiety. "Some of them don't believe you were born blind. They want to ask your parents." I was indignant, "But you've known me all my life, you *know* I was born blind!" Self-important, they hurried on with their Pharisee-appointed task.

Sure enough, reaching home I found my mother. She was fretting anxiously, gathering her shawl about her. "Oh, son," she said when I appeared, "what have you told them?" "The truth mother, what else? I was blind; this man Jesus gave me my sight. Why aren't they leading us in psalms of praise instead of all this arguing? Don't they want to know?" "I'll tell you why," said one of my neighbors, appointing himself the expert on religious matters. "The leaders have already said this Jesus is a sinner because he heals on the Sabbath. They've said anyone who says he's the Messiah will be put out of the synagogue." Even my father drew back at this. "I told you," he said, looking at me. "Come son, we must go and face them."

Back we went through the streets. A trail of people joined us, passing the story back and forth. People pointed at me and retold the arguments. My patience was running out. What did it matter which day a miracle of such wonder happened? We should only be thanking God for his grace beyond human limitations and understanding. Why couldn't they see?

A crowd was gathered at the temple: more pointing and whispering and arguing. A Pharisee stepped forward as my parents were led in. "Are you the parents of this man?" he asked. "We are," they answered, standing before the crowd as though condemned of some wrongdoing. "And is he the one who was born blind?" "He is," they answered without looking at me, as though I were guilty of some crime. "How then does he now see?" the Pharisee demanded, as if they might suddenly admit to some false testimony.

My mother was so afraid of these men. They represented a God she had tried to placate, a system she had obeyed without questioning. It was my father who answered, ensnared by the threat of exclusion from a system that had defined his life. He knew only submission to authorities he assumed were worthy. "We know that this is our son, and that he was born blind; but how he now sees we do not know, nor do we know who opened his eyes. Ask him; he is of age, he will speak for himself." I stared at my father, but he would not meet my eyes. Why could he not stand in the obvious truth?

The crowd was hushed as the Pharisee gestured for me to step into the center. I could see he was trying to maintain his dignity, struggling to show himself to be an authority who could speak the final word. "Give God the praise;" he instructed me," we know that this man is a sinner." I spoke up then—what did their rank and rules have to do with me? "Whether he is a sinner, I do not know," I said. "One thing I know, that though I was blind, now I see." He couldn't resist one more attempt at making me and everyone else agree to his way of seeing. "What did he do to you? How did he open your eyes?"

I was not trapped by the systems and authorities as my parents were. An outsider and a blind beggar I had been. But now I could see. And I saw the games, the power play, and the resistance to another way of seeing. I let go of ever being an insider. I answered him back. "I already told you, and you would not listen. Why do you want to hear it again? Do you too want to become his disciples?"

Angry now, the leader spat out, "You are his disciple, but we are disciples of Moses. We know that God has spoken to Moses, but as for this man, we do not know where he comes from." Their small-mindedness was declared. Wasn't it their responsibility to find out about anyone who might know our God? But they could not step outside their systems. I saw their blindness to other possibilities.

I felt the strength of my own conviction, my own visibility as I proclaimed my faith before them all. "Why, this is a marvel! You do not know where he comes from, and yet he opened my eyes. We know that God does not listen to sinners, but if anyone is a worshiper of God and does his will, God listens to him. Never since the world began has it been heard that anyone opened the eyes of a man born blind. If this man were not from God, he could do nothing."

At this the leader's temper broke. "You're the one who is the sinner. You were born in utter sin, and would you teach us?" And they physically pushed me out of the temple.

I went on my way, an outsider again. It was clear the Pharisees were declaring to everyone that my blindness was proof of my guilt. But a strange exhilaration had risen within me. I knew myself visible. I was more visible than my parents. I knew myself to be free. I was freer than the Pharisees. I was open to a God who broke the rules and through our categories to draw us into light and beauty and joyful freedom. I laughed out loud as I strode down streets I had once shuffled along. Ah, God of the blue sky, God of light, God of seeing, may I never be caught by the narrow rules. May I ever be an outsider if it means I can know you.

Days passed and I began to gain more understanding of the fear and submission my parents had exhibited. Now that I could see, I wanted to contribute to the needs of the family. I wanted to learn skills that would give me a future, maybe marriage and a family of my own. But the news had got around about me. My parents were concerned that the Pharisees had declared me guilty and cast me out. Others were not willing to associate with me. When I offered to work or asked to learn, some shunned me. They simply turned their backs and refused to speak with me.

I began to discover a side of my city I had not known. It was not just those with disabilities who couldn't work. I met another kind of outcast, unwanted due to questionable parentage or crimes or defiance of the establishment. They had a rough camaraderie among them; I began to seek out any who may long, as I did, to know the God who could meet us outside of the rules.

I was sharing some food one day with a group of men gathered at the edge of a marketplace to set out their wares. The talk
had turned to reports of Jesus. He spoke of God calling us to justice
and compassion. The gossip was that he'd said the Pharisees were
too busy obeying the tiniest of possible rules but missing the real
meaning. "Exactly!" I thought. "They cannot see what is before
their eyes. But this Jesus really sees."

I suddenly remembered what he had said that first day, before
I understood anything: "While I am in the world, I am the light
of the world." I began to explain this to the men, when I became
aware of a group of people behind me, listening. I turned to check
whether they would be likely to reprimand us for our ideas. As I
did so, one of them looked at me keenly, observing me the way
some people did when they had known me previously. The silence
in our conversation lengthened, and then the man spoke directly
to me, "Do you believe in the Son of Man?" The way he asked the
question made me wonder at his meaning. He seemed to be questioning my understanding of some deep truth, as you might talk
about the meaning of life, or what God is like.

I was drawn to him, even as I questioned what he meant.
"And who is he, sir, that I may believe in him?" Rather than explain himself and who he was, he simply gazed penetratingly at
me. "You have seen him," he said, then paused and smiled at me
as I tried to grasp what he was saying beneath his simple words.
"And," he added slowly, quietly, "it is he who speaks to you." As he
spoke I suddenly recognized his voice. That same quiet voice that
had said to me, not so long ago, but in a different life, "What is it
that you want?"

I stared, taking in what I had only sensed in him last time.
There was the quiet strength, the compassion, and the deep inten-
tional purpose that seemed to lift me to the highest place I could
imagine. No wonder he had said he was the light of the world.

I knelt at his feet—I did not care who saw. "Lord, I believe," I
said. He lifted me up and put an arm across my shoulders, drawing
me into a fellowship I did not understand. He declared to the group
who was following our exchange in silence: "For judgment I came

into this world, that those who do not see may see, and those who see may become blind." Obviously, some of the gathering crowd now realized who I was. I heard whispers about blindness and the temple and Pharisees. And there, watching attentively, were some Pharisees, obviously familiar with this man. One of them asked loudly, "Are we also blind?"

An hour before I would have been wary, sensing an implicit criticism. Now Jesus, his arm still across my shoulders, holding me in mute inclusion, answered him directly, "If you were blind, you would have no guilt; but now that you say, 'We see,' your guilt remains." In his answer to the Pharisees, he was giving me my answer: you are not guilty; you are included. I knew at that moment that he too saw himself as an outsider. He was the light of the world, but lived outside its petty systems. His light showed up the darkness and the blindness and the refusal to believe. From that moment I knew I would never be an outsider again, that I was accepted into something much greater. My eyes searched the faces of the men and women who were with him and I could see that they also knew this secret, the secret of another kingdom.

Mary's Reflection on the Man Born Blind

I wasn't there the day Jesus healed the man born blind. The others told me how Jesus had come across this man and then sent him away to wash the clay from his eyes. That was the last they had seen of him. It was only later that we heard he'd been thrown out of the temple for the way he spoke to the Pharisees.

I was there though, when Jesus went searching for him. Jesus wanted to find him, to make sure his healing had not isolated him from worship, to see if he was finding a way forward in his new life. Not many were brave enough to stand up to the Pharisees, especially over Jesus' identity. It wasn't too hard to find him. The story of his healing and his banishment from the temple was rumored through the streets of Jerusalem. We went back to the corner where he used to beg and asked where he might be. We found him sitting among a motley, disenfranchised lot, by the look of them. We stood and listened to the conversation: part complaint about the system and power, part longing for a better way and a deeper community. The once-blind man was voicing the search for something more. Jesus looked straight at him and asked him what he believed in.

I watched his face as he tried to articulate the deep longing that I once struggled to express. How do you speak what you hardly understand, what you sense as a deep gnawing within? As they talked, I saw the question enter his eyes and give way to slow recognition. It is hard to describe the dawning of joy that lit up his face, the wonder and gratitude that followed, the adoration that he expressed as he knelt. As Jesus lifted him and put an arm across his shoulder, something shifted. It was as though he had found the family he belonged to but had never known.

I was present once when a young man met his grandfather for the first time. His own father had left the family home and traveled far, marrying a foreign woman and dying there. His son had grown and returned, looking for any remaining extended family. I happened to be in their home when the young man was shown in. In spite of the forty years between them, the family likeness was unmistakable. I watched the young man recognize it in his grandfather and call this "his family." This was his home and something made him whole in that instant.

I was reminded of this as I watched Jesus put his arm across the man's shoulders. The look on the man's face changed. "This is where I belong, this is who I belong to:"
Bone of my bone and blood of my blood.
No other kin matter, it is you I am part of.
Your people shall be my people and your God shall be my God.
Even cast out I am not alone.
Even rejected I am known.
Seen and known.
You made me visible.
You gave me sight, to see as I am seen.
To see this world as you see it.
I am yours and you are mine, so be it.

I used to watch his face as he drank in Jesus' teaching. We stayed in Jerusalem some time after that. The once-blind man, full of the excitement of his new life, used to stay with us as much as he could. He wanted to follow Jesus anywhere, but Jesus told him to make a life for himself right there amongst those he knew and those, in his new-found vitality, he was befriending. When he heard this, his face fell and some confusion passed across it. Later, when we were sharing food and conversation, I asked him quietly what was troubling him about staying. Animated, he talked first about his new understandings of God and the kingdom way.

After a while he paused, looked at me questioningly, and began to tell me about his family. We had heard the story about how his parents had sidestepped the Pharisees' questions. Was that his problem? No, he told me thoughtfully, it wasn't really that. He was concerned about his mother. She had always been a woman who kept the laws very carefully; now she was becoming even more rigid, fearful, and anxious. He paused for a time, and then asked me, "Would you go and see her? You know Jesus so well and you understand the kingdom and how it fits with all our laws and regulations. Do you think you could help her understand? Help her trust God more?"

I wasn't sure that talking to her would make any difference, but, seeing his obvious disquiet, I told him I would see if she would talk to me about her fears. She seemed to be afraid even of him, he explained. His presence might catch the attention of the authorities and implicate her, so his cousin became my escort.

His mother agreed to see me. A few days later, we sat in a concealed corner of the house. At first she said little, glancing around as if afraid others were listening. But as I told her something of my own journey and the change in my own life, she became more still, beginning to reveal glimpses of her own questions and doubts. I visited her several times, and gradually she came to trust me with her story and its interlacing fears. I've retold it here, as it exemplifies the choice Jesus left with people. In the end, they had to ask the question, "Who is God and what is God like?"

10

The Cruelty of Dogma, the Fear of Freedom

The Blind Man's Mother

The Mother's Story

I REMEMBER THE WONDER of the birth of each of my children, the wonder of their perfection. I had such joy at examining each finger and toe, the tiny embodiment of humanity. So perfect, I thought, as I stroked the warm head, felt the body nestle into mine. I had carried him inwardly; now I held his warmth against my own body, this little being breathing its own life. Oh, the joy of seeing the limbs I had felt press from within, the face of a life, the mine-and-not-mine. Motherhood offered the possessive rapture of cradling my own little one in my arms, the delight in feeling him nuzzle at my breast, the gift of nurturing him with the certainty of sustenance and comfort. Through me, he discovered a world that is safe and enfolding.

1. John 9:18–23.

I knew from my firstborn, the delight of seeing his eyes begin to focus on mine. He followed bright cloth as he learned to watch movement. We shared the unspoken intimacy of eyes held while he was sucking at my breast.

But with the second one, this did not come. I remember my first inklings of fear, when his eyes did not flinch from light, follow movement, or seek my face bent over him in protection. I hid the creeping shame, the horror of potential blindness from others, willing it to change. Surely my intuition was wrong. How could a blind one survive in this world? Deeper, more troubling questions swirled inside me. How could this be? God of justice, how could this be? What have I done to deserve this? What sins have we committed? My husband is a good man—what do I not know? God, what of my imperfection do you hold against me? I had tried to keep the law, honor the elders, do right and good, become just. Oh, God of the Law, what have I not done, that this should be visited on me, that my son should be blind?

I hid it for days before the others noticed, the terror growing within me. I was horrified at my own contradictory reactions. I had a desire to protect my son, to run away with him and live elsewhere, to give my life to protect him. And at the same time I felt a horror of him, almost hatred, for the shame he was bringing.

Into his adulthood, the darkness pushed against my mother-love. I was relieved every day when he went from the house to beg. He brought what little he could to the household. I was glad I did not have to watch those sightless eyes follow sounds—but never the light. Thirty years passed and I still felt the shame that one born of my body should be blind. The shame I carried was not only for having borne him, but for my own rejection of him. The shame that gnawed at my inner being was the worse for never being spoken. I heard it in the brittle edge of my voice when I hurried him on his way or in my coolness when I greeted his return. What kind of mother was I that blamed my son for the shame I carried?

I tried to make up for it. I did everything good I knew. I observed every jot and tittle of the law, every Sabbath, every feast day. I tried to prove over and over and over that I was righteous, that it was not my sin. Sometimes a doubt would creep into my side-vision. Could I really convince an all-seeing God that I was righteous? If God had seen my sin, had seen fit to visit such judgment on the offspring of my womb, how could I convince that God that I was righteous? But those thoughts led me only to darkness and confusion. I would quietly busy myself about the house, obeying the commandments with even more attention.

My husband and I never spoke of it. I feared he carried the same shame, and did not know how to broach it. And so there was isolation for each of us. We were stiff in our obedience, wooden in our shared religious observance. We worshipped as if God could never be satisfied, and yet we knew not what to do except to try and satisfy a law we did not understand. We lived in this split, a pretense, and yet we lived in obedience.

So, when my once-blind son arrived home that day, my mind reeled, my emotions jarred and split. I spun into chaos. He came in the door earlier than usual; immediately, I sensed something different in the way he held himself. I looked up questioningly at my son's face—and he looked at mine. For the first time ever, he looked at my face. In that first instant before fear overwhelmed my senses again, I knew the utter joy of what I had longed for these thirty years: his eyes met mine. His joy was evident. He took me in his arms and tried to dance with me. He shouted with delight as he recognized by sight objects he had only known by touch.

But all too soon I put together what had happened. How could he have been healed on the Sabbath? My joy was robbed by my fear. It all came to a head sometime later. I was in the house, cooking, and I heard shouts. At the sound of a crowd approaching, I busied myself. I was never one to join in a crowd. But it was my door that burst open, my son who shouted my name, my house the neighbors pushed into. Everyone spoke at once, and the fear rose in me. But before I could even speak, the words of the shouts began to register. I heard the words: "Jesus," "that charlatan," "the Pharisees," "expelled," "Sabbath."

The crowd gabbled on, pushing their way out again, a human tide carrying my son off to see the Pharisees. And I was left with my fear. What would the Pharisees say? It had been a Sabbath when he was healed. The healer was a charlatan. The healer? How could one heal someone born blind? I held my son's face and his laughter for a moment in my mind. Had I not longed for this? But my fear swamped me. What had happened? What would the Pharisees say? How could our son do this to us?

I busied myself with my cooking pots, trying to bring order into a world tipped upside down. Even as I thought that, a tiny inner voice whispered, "Isn't it tipped right side up?"

All too soon, the crowd was back. My husband was there, calling me to come. We were swept along to the temple, surrounded by people jabbering of healing and the Sabbath, of a man who was supposed to be a prophet but couldn't be. I clung to my husband's arm and kept my eyes on the ground, the clanging voices jarring my thoughts. My fear was rising and I was silently calling out to the God who protects the righteous. But was I righteous? My hidden shame told me no. I hardly dared to look at the men who stood in judgment.

In the sudden silence, an authoritarian voice asked us, "Is this your son?" And there, indeed, was our son. He was so radiant, I dared not meet his eyes. I looked quickly away because I did not know how to respond to that joy, undiminished by the harsh voices of the Pharisees and the babble of the crowd.

Then came a call for silence and the question again: "Is this your son? You say he was born blind, how is it then that he can now see?" And in the hush, everyone waiting for us to answer, I did not know how to speak or what to say. My husband found a way. "We know that he is our son, and that he was born blind. But how he came to see, we do not know. He is of age, ask him." Even as I felt the relief, I knew the betrayal in his answer, too. We did not stand with our son—we let him carry his own exclusion. But he refused to be condemned. He stood, tall and jubilant, "One thing I know—I was blind but now I see."

A tiny part of me was proud; I wanted to run and stand tall with him. "This is my son, he is not blind, God has not judged him, God has not judged us. God affirms him!" But I was too afraid to move. I grew even more fearful as he stood up to them, contradicted them, even mocked them. Oh, my son, not this way!

Predictably, they put him in his place. The more they plunged in the knife, the more my old wound reopened. "You were born and brought up in sin, and would you teach us?!" they shouted. And they expelled him from the temple.

My old horror came back. My husband and I shrank and hurried out, heads down, silent. But my son, my tall, upright, insightful son, hurried up behind us and called us to see what he had seen. "Unless the man came from God, he would not be able to do such a thing!"

So stark before me is the choice I have always turned from. Will I believe in a God of judgment or a God who gives freedom? And I am too afraid to answer.

Mary's Reflection

When she had finally named all of this, she wept and clung to my hand begging me to help her answer her own deep question. She knew my answer already. I sat with her as she tried to find the courage to begin a different life. I visited her once more before we left Jerusalem. Threats of stoning and arrest had begun to follow us, and my own fears of darkness were closing in.

11

Letting Go Riches

Zacchaeus[1]

WE LEFT JERUSALEM FOR some weeks. We all breathed more easily far away from the temple authorities, and I'm sure some of
the others, like me, secretly hoped we would not go back at all.
Jesus' rich teaching was full of stories; some were sharply clear in
their criticism of the religious leaders, and all were profound in
their description of the kingdom and reflection of the ways of the
Father. And he kept telling us that he must go to Jerusalem, that he
would be tortured and killed. We simply didn't want to believe it.
We couldn't see any purpose in it at all.

Jesus' ministry was touching people from all classes and parts
of life. Sometimes there was a real sense that we lived together
in the kingdom of God: rich and poor, educated and unlearned,
beggar and landowner. Though we often felt the darkness closing
in, our traveling band shared many bright stories and moments
of joy, laughter, and intimacy. One of the unexpected, humorous
stories was that of Zacchaeus, the chief tax collector. Who would

1. Luke 19:1–10.

97

ever have thought he would be interested in the traveling spiritual teacher? What use would he have for a kingdom whose riches had nothing to do with money?

We neared Jerusalem, taking the road through Jericho. As always, there were delays: someone asked for healing, others invited us to a meal or to stay for the night. We decided to stay in Jericho, and then take that long rocky road towards Jerusalem.

Here's Zacchaeus' story as he told it to me years later.

Zacchaeus' Story

I had heard of him before he came. Jesus was reportedly a man not intimidated by the authorities. He spoke his words whatever their reactions, even despite the murmurings to see him killed. He stood up to the moneychangers in the temple; he drove them out for a few days, the rumors said. He was a man unimpressed by the power of the rulers. But going by the stories, I was pretty sure he was not a rebel, either. The rebels, the Zealots—I don't go along with their pie-in-the-sky. Who could hope to overthrow the Romans? Anyone with half an eye can see the power they carry. But somehow, they said, Jesus saw right through the might-is-right and called people to something else. They said he hung around with the poor, the down-and-outs. Obviously, he was not impressed with wealth.

That's what first caught my attention, because I was not impressed with riches either. Not any more I wasn't. But I saw how many people were. Even when I could see in their eyes that they didn't like me, they still cowered. They were still subservient, obsequious, and impressed with my wealth. But I had lived that life too long; it had palled. It was all dinners and snobbery and superiority. Now I saw through its lies and false promises. It had provided a buffer for me against the ups and downs of life. But it had buffered me from true life, as well. I hungered for something more.

Was he really a prophet? A seer? Could he really see through the facade of lies people throw up against life? I wanted to look at him and see: was he just another charlatan, trickster, entertainer, slick storyteller, or, maybe, idealistic dreamer? Or, was he real?

Reports came from Jerusalem, from Galilee, and then from beyond Galilee. Crowds followed him there. I even considered following the stories, but I guess I didn't have enough hope that he would measure up. People will run after anyone when they're afraid, desperate, hanging in crisis.

But then he was nearby—in Jericho, they said—a rabble at his heels, as always. He was on his way to Jerusalem to observe the Passover feast. I decided it was worth the effort to go and see for myself. I tried to get to the house where he was staying, but there was a crowd. Sick people and poor people gathered around the door, some had even been sleeping outside all night. Short as I am, I couldn't even see him when he appeared, but I caught snatches of what he said as people in the crowd repeated it to each other. But I heard enough to confirm it was worth trying to hear more. As I listened to the talk around me, I gleaned he was heading for Jerusalem that day—and it was obvious which road he would take out of town.

I decided I could go ahead and wait from some vantage point where I could see him. I walked up the dusty road looking for a likely spot to stand. Then I spied the sycamore tree, its branches overhanging the road. I'd be close enough to see him, even to hear a little of what he was saying as he passed underneath. I knew I'd look pretty silly perched out there. But I also knew I already wasn't a favorite among the townspeople. I no longer cared what people said.

I climbed up to the lower branches and waited. As the day wore on, I thought about what had brought me to that place of wanting truth and seeking meaning beyond security and comfort. I even admitted that the relationships I had were superficial and shallow. I had driven people away in my pursuit of money, and then tried to impress them with my possessions. I no longer wanted a life of comfort that cost me everything else. As I mused, I found I was hoping desperately that this Jesus saw a reality beyond mine. My silly reality of possessions and security that most of the world seemed to be scrambling after.

Finally, I heard the sounds of a crowd, children running ahead and laughing. Then people began appearing, helping a sick person into position for a chance to touch him. How must it be, I wondered, to have to wade through this mass of people to get where he wanted to go?

Some boys saw me in the tree and decided to climb up, too. In the end, there were five of us perched in the tree, talking about what we'd heard. One of the boys was big-eyed as he told of the miracles he had heard about. "But what does he say?" I questioned them. "That's what I want to know." They were vague. He says that we should look after each other, that there's a kingdom where everybody can be happy, that we don't have to fight each other. They each contributed something they'd heard.

At last he came, slowly. He paused to talk to a sick one here, pick up a child there, exchange a word or two with an elderly one. My first reaction was disappointment. He was just an ordinary man, nothing special. Certainly he was not a Samson or a Solomon striding through the crowd. But as he got closer and I could see the expressions on people's faces, I began to hope again. Somehow, there was a peace about him. People's expressions changed: strain and worry became rest and even delight.

As I watched, I dared to believe what I had hoped—he lived what he said, he treated all with compassion, he really did believe that peace among men was possible. And at last he was close enough for me to hear his words. His were simple words: concern for someone's fear, an answer to a question about the law. At last he stopped and looked up at the boys calling out to him from our tree, laughing with them at our perch. Something in his laughter warmed my heart. The freedom of his laughter drew me like nothing else. Suddenly, I wanted to be able to laugh like that, as though nothing in the world mattered at all.

His eyes turned to me. I could see him take me in. And the silence spread as people noticed where he was looking. The stillness in him stilled my heart. I felt as though he knew me, as though I was looking into the face of an old friend, an uncle who long ago had loved me. We just looked at each other. Inside, I wondered what people must think of this long, slow, silent look. But it didn't matter. All that mattered was that he kept looking. He did not sneer at me, nor cringe, nor stare me down. He just gave me a long upraising look that seemed to say, "I know you, too. I know what you deeply, secretly want and it's yours for the asking." The meeting of our eyes conveyed all that. As I held on to the branch, I was stripped to my inner being. Once, it would have scared me witless to lose sense of the expensive clothes that declared my wealth, to be caught perching in a tree with some street ragamuffins, and to be seen as the lonely, empty man that I truly was. None of that mattered, if only I never lost this sense of deep Life I was glimpsing.

"Come on down," he said, "I want to come to your home." It was as though he had offered me a place at a banquet where all were welcomed and equally accepted. I wanted nothing more than this feast among brothers. Crashing in on that vision, then, came my rich, ostentatious house with its pillars and fountains and Roman decor. My house was not the place for a feast of equals. And I wanted, more than anything, to feast among brothers, even in a humble, one-bedroom hut or out on the hillside open to the sky. A sliver of memory flashed through me: camping under the stars as children at the feast of tabernacles, when we made our booths of branches and ate and laughed together. That's what I wanted more than all my wealth and comfort and security. And here was this man offering it to me.

I knew in that moment I could have it—but it would cost me everything. And it seemed like a fair exchange. I can only say it was a moment of deep grace, of vision into the Reality of the world. That release of everything that does not matter is the only way to claim all that does matter. And as his eyes held mine, I let everything go.

Even as I clambered down from the tree, past the boys hand-over-hand around me, totally undignified in my haste, I could hear people in the crowd muttering. "A sinner." "Doesn't he know?" "Cheating people of honest wages." I felt no animosity—it was as though they spoke of someone else, someone I had once been long ago. As I jumped the last couple of feet to the ground, Jesus held out a hand of welcome. I tripped over my words in greeting: "Look, Lord! Here and now I give half of my possessions to the poor, and if I have cheated anybody out of anything, I will pay back four times the amount." "I know," he said, and smiled at me. I knew the feast of brothers had begun.

Mary's Reflection

Zacchaeus is still a rich man. He is one of those people who can turn anything to gold. However much he gives away, somehow he can still make more. He's no longer a tax collector, though. He started a business and it obviously flourished.

When I arrived at his big house I wondered if he had forgotten the day he climbed the sycamore and met Jesus. Maybe he had gone back on his word. People had told me otherwise, but here at his house I wondered. A servant had shown me to a seat on the airy verandah. Would he even come and talk to me?

I needn't have been concerned. He came hurrying down the stairs, a little, bent man full of vibrant energy. His arms outstretched, he wore a beaming smile on his face. He wouldn't hear me out until he'd ordered drinks and settled me comfortably. Even when I told him what I had come to hear, he stopped me and said, "But tell me your story first. How are you faring after all these years?" Only after he had listened to me and asked of the welfare of the others, did he tell me his memories of that day. He laughed joyfully as he described climbing up into the tree, waiting there until Jesus stopped and told him to come down. He was obviously delighted in people knowing what he used to be, a hated tax collector. He clearly and permanently saw himself as one of the lowest, yet one of the redeemed. His status and his riches were of no consequence, except when they could help other people find God and find community.

As we talked, a couple of little boys, his grandchildren I presumed, came in and climbed up into his lap. He tousled their hair and gave them a drink from his cup and fruit from the dish between us on the table. When they ran off into the garden he told me their story. Their mother had been a prostitute with no family to take her in. She was not his relative at all, but one of the flow of people who came and lived with him. His opulent house had become a haven for many, a place of safety where they could begin their lives over.

12

A Woman's Priestly Gift

The Woman Who Anointed His Head[1]

IT WAS THE GATHERING darkness that led to the incident I want to tell you about in my next story. All of us had begun to feel the threats, the possibility of death, or of fighting for our lives, depending on the way we understood it all. We had been so relieved to be out of Jerusalem; we were breathing more easily and not jumping at shadows. But Jesus insisted we return. There were disagreements about it and more arguments than usual. Susanna and I pulled back from some of the others—our presence only made the short tempers shorter.

I've already told you that it was my friend Susanna who first introduced me to Jesus. It was she who invited him to my home to draw me back into life from the deathly place I inhabited. It was because of her that I came up with the idea of traveling with Jesus and the men who accompanied him. Then we could be learning from him, listening to his stories, watching his interactions with

1. Matt 26:6–13, Mark 14:3–9.

the people, discussing the possibilities he raised, and arguing about what it all meant in our real, everyday lives.

I was the romantic one, always ready for adventure, idealistic in my dreams of the future. I was sure that anything could happen if Jesus was part of it. Susanna was older, more practical, and more grounded, but she took my dreams seriously and tempered them with reality. Later, it was she who helped the early communities embody the living teaching of Jesus, talk through differences, and resolve conflict. And her faith was grounded in the scriptures, linking the old ways with the new.

When I came up with the idea of gathering stories, she encouraged me, but she would not come with me. She was too involved in the growing communities of those of us who followed the way of Jesus. She was always ready to hear the stories I gathered, sometimes prompting my memory, sometimes sharing how she had experienced it.

She wanted her story told, too. "But you must let me tell it in my way, Mary. I want to be able to tell about your part in it, but it in my own way." The anointing of Jesus' head, soon before his death, marked a highlight in her life. It's not a story often told, though Jesus' himself said, "I tell you the truth, wherever this gospel is preached throughout the world, what she has done will be told, in memory of her."[2] When it is heard, its significance is often missed. But Susanna and I knew. She always held it as a sacred memory, a sacred interchange between her and her Lord.

Susanna's Story

My name is Susanna. I was a companion to Jesus and his disciples, to Mary Magdalene and Joanna.[3] You don't need to know much about my background. I was from a wealthy family and I had married a wealthy man who died after our children were married. I

---

2. While this is said in Matt 26:13 and Mark 14:9, neither gospel mentions her name, and the story of Mary of Bethany anointing Jesus' feet (John 12:1–8) tends to overshadow it.

3. Luke 8:3

was in the unusual position: an independent woman, free in how I lived my life, with money to draw on and a family to return to. So from early on, Mary, Joanna, and I traveled with Jesus.

I watched Mary sometimes as she listened to Jesus. She was a beautiful woman, but her utter, heart-deep love was also written on her face. I would watch as she drank in his teaching; it was her very sustenance. I had known her when she was ill, when her face was drained and pale. The contrast was absolute. As she listened to him, it seemed that her essential being was renewed by the very breath of God. A glow would spread over her face, a radiance into her eyes. She would turn to me, her eyes alight, and say something like, "Would you *listen* to this! Isn't it water to the depths of your being?" For her it always was. Even when he spoke in riddles or in dark ways about the rulers or the things to come, she looked as though she was in on the secret, as though she physically saw the kingdom of which he spoke.

I didn't always understand. Jesus spoke so often in parables and while I enjoyed simply listening to his story-telling, I knew I often didn't hear the deeper meaning. I was always glad when someone asked him to explain. More than once he said to me, "Are you also so dull of heart that you do not understand?" and I would have to confess that I was. I wished I was more like Mary. I think the long dark night of her sickness and the transformation Jesus wrought in her had somehow given her glimpses of heaven and hell. She understood the spiritual kingdom much better than I.

But I wanted to understand, and I learned not to be afraid to ask for explanations, either of her or of Jesus. Even though Jesus would name it as dullness of heart, he would patiently explain again and again the kingdom he was inviting us to live in, the intimate relationship with God as Abba Father. Gradually, over those three years I seemed to grasp more often what he was saying. It wasn't that I wasn't educated or intelligent enough. Dullness of heart he called it—it was an inability to see with the spirit. As I journeyed with him, I tried to put into practice what he was teaching us. I watched as he went off to talk to God alone; I listened as he explained to us how to pray. And I too began to rise early and sit out on the hillside, lakeshore, or quiet housetop in the presence of the Father he spoke of with such authority and intimacy.

Of course, Jahweh had always been a part of my life. I had always enjoyed the festivals and prayers in the synagogue. But this way of being with God changed something in my heart and gradually brought me to a place of finding the presence of this God. I found the spirit-breath within, one with whom I could converse, and know a response. So sometimes as Jesus told his parables I would feel a rush of recognition. Oh yes, I know this God he is speaking of; I know this mercy, this kindness, this call to celebration.

I remember, it was towards the end and his stories and directives were becoming stronger, sometimes shocking. The rich young man came with such excitement, running to ask how he would live his life, only to be told to sell everything. He couldn't take it. In the early days, I would have wanted to run after him and soften what Jesus had said. Surely, it was okay to just give a tithe; Jesus didn't really mean it that strongly. Mary would be the one in those days to take me aside and explain—with shining eyes she would tell me that Jesus meant exactly what he said. And gradually I came to know that if I didn't get it, I should sit with it in the presence of the Father at dawn or hold it gently as I fell asleep, trusting that more understanding would come.

So, when that young man came and went, and the men began a discussion about riches, I knew that wasn't really the point. The real issue was whatever it was that hindered me from deep heart response to God. You might think that because I was well off, I felt secure and didn't really face the challenge. But no, I remember thinking at the time: "I *could* give it all away! Now, I *could* give it all away!" I had tasted of the riches of this God and I could give away anything that stopped me from being able to live with that.

A significant conversation with Jesus also helped me. We had been walking from one village to another and had stopped to rest and eat in some shade by the path. We'd fallen into quiet conversation. He asked me how it was for me, traveling with them. I'd said that the absence of my usual comforts wasn't much of an issue for me. He was silent for a moment, looking at me quietly, before he asked what *was* an issue for me. I knew by then not to answer his questions too quickly. He was always putting his finger on anything that held us back from the presence of God. I sat in silence looking inwards. "It's what people think of me that matters," I had to answer. "I want everyone to think well of me." He looked at me as though he would give the world to see me walk in freedom. "What a trap that one is," he said gently. "You will need to let it go if you want to be part of the kingdom."

I came to realize that he asked everyone the same question— in different ways and in different forms—What's keeping you from seeing the kingdom? What's stopping you knowing the father? What's keeping you locked into legalism and self-righteousness? What's preventing forgiveness? What's hindering your trust? It dawned on me that he was not just a teacher and a healer, but also a priest—one who led others into the presence of God, if only they would come. I began to see everything he said in a new light. This was not a call to a sacrificial life—although it was that. It was, first and most importantly, a call to know this God who gave with such exceeding generosity. He gave rain on the just and unjust, trees that produced way more seeds than could ever take root, stars that lit the night sky like jewels, dainty field flowers here today and gone tomorrow. He was the father who ran, skirts lifted, to meet his exiled son. He was the generous provider of the hundred and fifty gallons of wedding wine, the father of the bridegroom inviting all the waifs and strays, the God who stooped to earth as a naked baby. I began to find myself in tears as he told story after story. He was always speaking of the kingdom, but I began to realize he was mostly trying to help us know the King. He was taking us to the Mother-Father God who wept over us with compassion, knelt at our feet to draw us into freedom, and gave recklessly and extravagantly even to the death.

It was Mary who spoke to me of his death. "Do you notice he keeps talking about his death?" she said quietly one day. We were preparing food together while the men returned from preaching in nearby villages. I *had* noticed, but had pushed it away. "The

others push it away too, you know." she said. "He's trying to prepare us. Trying to show us it will happen, has to happen, maybe.
Oh, Susanna, do you think it *has* to happen?" I didn't know what
she meant. She tried to explain, "He says a prophet must go to
Jerusalem to die. He says the son of the landowner will come back
and they will kill him. He said he must be killed so he can be raised
to life. Susanna, whatever does he mean?"

I didn't know how to answer her either, but I saw how deeply
troubled she was. I began to tell her of my ponderings about him
being a rabbi, a healer, and a priest. "Why a priest?" she wanted
to know. "Well, not like the priests in the temple, the Levites,
but a priest by divine gift—like Aaron was. He is one who stands
between the people and God, who stands in the holy place so
that we can go through him to touch God, because he's in God's
presence." She looked intrigued. "A new kind of priest," she mur-
mured. "He's been that to me," I continued. "I didn't even imagine I could know God's presence till he showed me how. And now
it's life and breath to me." I could see she understood, but then
she frowned: "But does he have to actually die to do that?" she
queried. I didn't know how to answer her, and the conversation
moved on to other matters.

I continued to come back to the idea: Jesus, a special kind of
priest who has come to bring us into the presence of God. A priest
knows what needs to be done for us to enter the holy of holies.
Mary's question remained: "Does he have to die?" I didn't know
how to answer that, but I became more and more convinced that
he would die. The rumors of the Pharisees' hatred were becoming more frequent. The sadness deepened on Jesus' face when he
was sitting in silence. He was more agitated when he spoke of "the
signs of the times." And then came his terrible outpouring of anger
against the Pharisees, when he called them hypocrites and vipers.
I knew they would never forgive him after that, even though he
ended by weeping over Jerusalem. I had to admit he was like an
olden day prophet, pouring out his vision of the kingdom and
contrasting it with the way we as a people have chosen to live. A

prophet was so often killed by the religious leaders in olden times. But the image of the priest stayed with me.

We traveled up to Jerusalem for the Passover. Some of the men tried to persuade him not to go, but they finally had to come along. Thomas so aptly put it, "Even though it means we die with him." We were back and forth a bit between Jerusalem and Bethany. Martha, of course, always made us welcome. And there were others there who had come to know us well and welcomed us into their homes. Simon the Leper was one of them. He wasn't really a leper, but a disfigurement on his face made him looked like one. He had been called that as a child and the name had stuck. He was a rich man and did not lack friends. In fact, his disfigurement seemed to have made him especially accepting, especially welcoming to the stranger. We stayed in his house on and off and he often invited us for a meal when we were in the town.

I had been talking with Mary about how we could respond to Jesus. He was clearly facing terrible opposition, but, as usual, many of the crowd, many of his close friends, just couldn't understand what he was trying to say. "What can we do?" I asked Mary in what turned out to be the final week together. "How can we show him that we love him, that we hear what he's saying, that we are with him?" She sat silent and a tear ran down her cheek. "I've been thinking again about him being a priest," I told her. "The one who gives sacrificially so his people can come to God."

A frown creased her forehead, and I glimpsed something of the pain she carried. "So what do you give a priest?" she asked. We sat in silence musing over the question. At last a thought struck me. "Well, at least we *recognize* him as a priest," I suggested. Her smile lit up her face. "What a lovely idea!" she responded, "To let him know you see! To let him know you understand what he's on about!" It was with her encouragement that I came up with the idea of anointing him, as one would anoint a priest.[4] "The precious

---

4. Exod 29:7, Take the anointing oil and anoint him [Aaron, the high priest] by pouring it on his head; Lev 8:12, He poured some of the anointing oil on Aaron's head and anointed him to consecrate him.

oil poured out on Aaron's head,"[5] we used to sing in the psalms on the way up to Jerusalem. "But, Mary, it should be another priest who does that!" She laughed aloud. "Since when did Jesus obey the letter of the law?" she asked. "That's what he's saying all the time. The Law is only a shadow. What's the Real?" I began to see what she was getting at. "That he's a priest in his Father's kingdom is the Real. That you too are a priest, that's Real." She laughed again. "A woman priest! He would love that! The kingdom of his Father where all who come enter into the Presence of the Living God. Yes, Susanna, you have to do it!"

We were to gather at Simon's the very next evening. I knew he would not turn me out for what might have seemed a mockery of the religious customs. Even if he didn't understand, I knew he would be patient and accepting. Some of the others wouldn't, I was sure of that. It didn't matter what they thought, I told myself. It matters only what Jesus thinks. It matters that he knows that we understand something of what he has been trying to show us. It matters that he knows that we see him, the presence of his Father, the one who has invited us into that holy place of deep relationship.

I went to buy anointing oil. I tried to buy the ingredients listed in the law: myrrh and cinnamon. Of course, I couldn't get it exactly right, but by then I had become very serious. It felt like a holy task, a truly sacred anointing of him. This was an anointing no traditional priest would ever make, and I wanted it to honor him, to name him in the eyes of heaven. With Mary's encouragement, I spoke to Simon, explaining we had a small ceremony at the end of the meal. He caught something of my solemnity and didn't ask me the details. He just nodded—as the host he would make a space for me.

The meal was generous and the various dishes kept appearing. Finally people stopped eating and Simon called for silence. He spoke out some of his own deep appreciation of Jesus and then he looked at me, inviting me with his eyes to stand with him. There was a silence as I stood and went to fetch the alabaster jar. I felt a trembling within me, but also a surge of joy. I knew that what I did

5. Ps 133:2.

signified something more profound than I could grasp and that somehow Almighty God *had* spoken to me heart and called me to this anointing. I did not dare to speak, fearing my voice would break, but silently I spoke the words of the psalm: the precious oil to consecrate the priest, poured on the head, running down on the beard. "Oh, God of the heavens," I prayed silently, "here is your priest. Here is the one who has drawn us into your presence by his life, by his living relationship with you. We recognize him as our priest."

There was a gasp from the others—they clearly understood the significance of what I'd done. Clearly some of them disagreed with my taking it upon myself to do it. The sacred silence was broken by a murmur of voices, quickly rising to a babble. Simon remained still behind me and Jesus turned his head to look up at me with a look I can hardly describe. It held gratitude, joy, pain, understanding. That look seemed to continue for minutes, although it was probably only moments. It soothed my beating heart and calmed any concern that I might displease him. All fear I had of what the others thought was gone. His silence eventually silenced the voices, the criticism. He turned back to them. "Leave her alone," he said. "She has done a beautiful thing for me. I tell you the truth, wherever the gospel is preached in all the world, what she has done will also be told in memory of her."

His words confirmed my deeper intuition that he was a priest, a priest of the Living God. Wherever his story is told, this also will be told: that he mediates a new way to come to God, a better covenant of profound grace and boundless mercy.

13

The End of Days,
the Beginning of Forever

Mary's Story of the Crucifixion[1]

OVER THE NEXT WEEK, the women of the group drew closer together in many ways. The men were reacting differently. Judas was particularly edgy—but then, we all were. We all felt under pressure. Some of the time Jesus seemed quite preoccupied, and at others he was most sensitive. He had always said things we did not understand, but that week everything he said seemed weighted with deeper meaning. The sense of foreboding became intense. Susanna and I would share notes about everything he said, and sometimes we asked Mary, Jesus' mother, to help us understand what was happening. She made it clear that she couldn't be sure either, but the deep sadness in her face told me she expected only further grief. We planned our Passover meal. It was clear that this was a focal point for Jesus. He was concerned about particular details: where we would share it, where we were staying. When we pressed him for an explanation, he would reiterate what he had said already. He

1. From Matt 27, Mark 15–16, Luke 23–24, John 20.

would be delivered over to the authorities and would die, but he would come to us again. How could we know what he meant by that? His solemnity forbade us to keep asking. So we prepared for the Passover and, if we could not be with him, we clung together, as if afraid some enemy would take us unawares.

Finally it was time for the meal. Before we ate, Jesus insisted on washing our feet. He came to each of us. I will never forget the tenderness of his hands and the compassionate love in his look as he finished drying my feet with the towel. I sat with tears running down my face, deeply aware that this was both a goodbye and an example of the way we were now to care for each other. At the beginning of the meal, when he broke the bread and said it was his body, I only knew he was telling us something deeply significant. As we have repeated that sharing of bread over and over down the years, it has never lost the feeling of that first time, the feeling that something was shifting in the way the world was constituted.

Even through the meal, we tried to get him to explain more. But the more he said, the less sense it seemed to make. I remember at some point in the meal he met my eyes as if trying to convey something profound, some mix of reassurance and deep agony. I wished with all my heart I could shield him from whatever was to come, yet I grasped that he had to go through with what was happening. He trusted himself to the Father, and we were to follow him in that as well. I determined that whatever happened, we would stay as close to him as we could, being present if nothing else. Whatever I imagined, it did not come near to what actually unfolded over the next hours.

If you have heard anything of the story of Jesus you will have heard of his crucifixion. I can hardly bear to relate the details, even still, but let me tell you something of my experience. He wanted to take the men outside the city walls to the Mount of Olives where they slept sometimes while we women stayed within the city. Foolishly, I wanted to go with them. I did not want to let him from my sight, but he told me gently and firmly that I was not to come. It would only make it worse, he said, and asked me to stay with his mother. "You will be able to come soon enough," he assured me.

"Now rest so you are ready for what is ahead." I begged Andrew to send someone to fetch us if anything happened, and he too tried to persuade me to keep safe with the other women. We had to let them leave, dreading the summons that we knew would come sooner or later.

I slept fitfully that night. Whenever I woke, I knew that one of the others was awake, too. It was as though between us we kept vigil, not knowing what the vigil was. The next morning Andrew came as he had promised. His story was garbled; he had clearly been terrified by the events of the night. He told us that they had gone to Gethsemane to pray and had slept a little until a band of soldiers came. The soldiers had surrounded Jesus and taken him away. Peter had tried to fight, he said. Whatever my differences with Peter, I loved him in that moment for his reckless defense of Jesus. But Jesus had told him to put away his sword and had given himself up to them. Andrew told us, with shame, that he had run away then, and had not dared to come back into the city until there were enough people coming in and out of the gates that he could return surreptitiously. He had tried to find out what was happening without drawing attention to himself.

All he knew was that Jesus had gone before the high priest, and was now before the council. They were planning to take him to Pilate, next. "To Pilate?" we questioned him. They were obviously trying to get the death sentence or they would have dealt with it themselves.

We hurried through the streets to stand with a gathering crowd outside the praetorium. The memory of that day is a confused tangle of images, with voices and shouts and jarring terror. At one point, Pilate appeared and asked the jabbering crowd if he should release Jesus. I remember that moment because it was like the eye of the storm. Everything was still and silent for less than a second and I dared hope for a tiny instant that he really might be released, that it would all be over, that we could get away from this horror. But then the voices rose, shouting for the release of Barabbas. I couldn't believe it. How could they? How could they?

Pilate went inside again. The crowd buzzed with excitement, as if they were making something glorious happen. The next image is of Jesus, standing beside Pilate, a purple robe around him. And even from our distance, I could see the thorns, a mockery of a crown. But more importantly, I noticed the stillness in him. He stood impassive, looking out over the crowd, as I had seen him look many times. He was neither afraid of them, nor taken in by their praise and adulation. Immediately came the shouts, "Crucify him! Crucify him!" I started screaming and trying to push forward through the crowd, but Susanna and Mary held me back. Mary took my face in her hands. "Look at me, child. Hold your peace. He could have left any time. You know that. He has given himself to this." She held my eyes till I nodded, then took me in her arms until my sobbing quieted. She spoke quietly, gently reminding me, "We are to be here with him. That is all. He knows we are here, keeping vigil." I remember thinking I would rather fight like Peter, but I knew that was not the way. In the midst of the raucous crowd I knew that our place was to be silent, to be present, and to hold the place of prayer. That was all.

At last it became clear that there was no way back, that they would crucify him on Golgotha's Hill. We decided to make our way towards it, to try and find a place beside the road so we could be visible as he passed. I remember how the hours seemed to drag and slow to a standstill. At other times it was all happening too fast and we could hardly take a breath before another horror. We did find a place on the road, and he did see us. He stopped to meet our eyes in passing; I still can hardly bear to think about it, the blood and torn flesh. And somehow we made our way to the place of crucifixion where we kept vigil, waiting and watching, holding each other for comfort and courage. John appeared, with other women of our group, and stood with us; others just passed by, or stopped to mock and shout abuse. I hated them all. I wished them all eternal damnation.

And when at last the sky darkened and the ground shook, I thought it was the end of the world—we deserved that it be so. We huddled on the ground and prayed and watched and waited. But the world did not end. Slowly it lightened again. And finally Jesus cried out, that terrible cry of desolation, "My God, my God, why have you forsaken me?" It seared through my body, throwing my inner darkness into chaos. Then at last, the terrible rasping breaths stopped, and he hung lifeless. And still we waited, and wept.

The other men crucified with him were still alive. The centurion stood guard. We stayed in that terrible place of torture and death, waiting, as if there were nothing left in the world to do. Toward evening I wondered if we would simply stay there on that bare hilltop, staring at its crosses against a meaningless sky, and wait for the world to truly end. But suddenly there was talk around us and Nicodemus and Joseph of Arimathea appeared with a linen shroud and spices and permission to take the body down. They lowered the body down to us and we carefully wrapped it, knowing that when the Sabbath was over we could return with more spices. We followed the men who carried his body to a garden tomb not far from Golgotha and watched them lay him there. We stumbled back through the streets to where we were staying. Someone gave me something hot and calming to drink and Mary insisted I drink it. At last I slept, in exhaustion and grief.

I woke in terrible bleakness. I remember sitting in the corner of a large room and watching people come and go. Some of the men came in for muted conversation, telling and retelling the events of the day before, piecing together the fragments of the story—who had said what, who had been where—until it culminated on that awful bare hill, overlooking a city that cast him out.

I half listened. Part of me tried to make any sense of it I could; part of me pulled back into an apathetic darkness. Mary and Susanna, my faithful friends, came and sat with me, made me eat and drink. Mary's face I remember, especially, because I wondered how she could stay so calm in the midst of this chaotic futility. "Mary," she reminded me more than once, "we are keeping vigil." But it meant nothing to me, and I shut my eyes and ears against it. Later in the day, when she reminded me that we would take more spices in the morning, I felt renewed interest. We agreed that at first light we would go together to the tomb where we had seen him laid.

I slept without herbs that night, but I knew, when I woke to a muffled cry more than once, that others too were having nightmares. We were each reliving our fears and terrors of the last week. I woke while it was still dark, but I could tell it must be dawn shortly. I couldn't wait any longer. I could feel the awful despair threatening to take over again, and I knew I must get up and do something. Pulling my cloak around me, I felt my way to where Mary had placed the spices. A whisper told me someone else was awake, but I didn't want to wait any longer. I only needed to be up and going, doing something, however small and meaningless.

It was light enough to find my way through the streets, and I pulled my cloak about my face and hurried, head down, with the flasks of spices and ointments. As I hastened toward the garden that held the tomb, I wondered how I could move the great round stone they had rolled over the opening. Would I be able to lever it along? I would try! If I couldn't move it, at least I could sit outside the tomb near his body—eventually someone would come and I could ask for help. But at least I would be as near to him as I could. "And yes, Mary," I thought, "I will keep vigil."

The early birds had begun to sing, and I remember wondering at them. Shouldn't all life have stilled at his death? I wanted even the birds to be in mourning. Part of me remonstrated at such folly. But no, I thought, he is the light of the world. And now the light of the world has been dimmed, extinguished, and we are left in darkness.

In the slow beginnings of dawn, I found my way to the garden entrance and followed the path that led down to where the tomb was. I suddenly realized that I was looking straight into the opening of the tomb with the stone already rolled to one side. Had someone come ahead of me, after all? Then I remembered a snatch of conversation from the day before, something about guards making sure no one would steal Jesus' body. At the time I had thought it stupidity, but now as I bent to look in I wondered if it could be true. There was no body there. I fell to my knees and wept, realizing how much I had longed for the comfort of touching him again.

As I knelt at the entrance to the tomb, trying to still my thoughts enough to make sense of what to do next, Mary and Joanna appeared behind me. "What have they done with his body?" I cried, as if they could somehow know. Joanna recalled something of the previous day's conversation and thought perhaps the men had come up with some plan to move his body after all. That was enough to give me hope again. Gathering my flasks, I ran ahead of them through the winding streets, pausing only to catch my breath as I opened the door.

I could make out Peter and John in low conversation. Interrupting them I blurted, "They have taken the Lord out of the tomb, and we do not know where they have laid him." They turned and stared at me, as if trying to ascertain if I was in my right mind. They turned to each other, and without another word, grabbed their cloaks, and made for the door. "No, wait!" I cried, but they had already left me behind, running back up the hill.

I trailed behind them. Clearly they didn't know of some other place the body could have been taken. Mary and Joanna, coming back, tried to persuade me to return with them, but I refused. I wanted to find out what John and Peter were going to do. Mary hesitated, about to say more, but she looked at me carefully and held her peace. I heard the men's voices as I rounded the last corner. Peter's voice was loud and questioning, John's quieter but with utter conviction. "He's alive, I tell you. He told us!" John's words made no sense to me. Peter, glancing up at me, hardly paused, "What are you talking about? How can you say that?" Peter was obviously in as much confusion as I was. I passed them, and went back to the tomb. What else could I do? I would keep vigil for him here, where I had last seen him.

I stood in the early morning stillness, hearing the birds sing as if the world had not changed, and my tears flowed again. Everything seemed surreal, as though nothing should be as it was before, and when I suddenly realized there were two men sitting in the tomb, it somehow didn't surprise me. One of them spoke to me, and I remember thinking his voice sounded familiar and yet foreign, as if I had heard the accent a long time ago. "Woman, why are you weeping?" he asked me gently. "Because they have taken away my Lord and I do not know where they have laid him," I answered tearfully.

Turning away, I saw someone else standing nearby, his back to the rising sun. I remember thinking again that the sun shouldn't continue to rise and set as if nothing had changed. He too asked me, "Woman why are you weeping?" I thought perhaps he was the gardener, and when he added, "Who are you looking for?" I begged him, "Sir, if you have carried him away, tell me where you have laid him, and I will take him away." Even as I said the words, I knew they didn't make sense, but they expressed my longing for him, for even his body. I wanted to take it where at least it would be safe. There was a brief silence, and then he spoke my name, "Mary," the way that only he could say it. In that instant, heaven and earth lurched back into harmony. "Teacher," I gasped and I was in his arms in a moment, clinging as if this dream too might shatter. He held me, and I will never forget the warmth of his body and the firmness of his touch. I had the sense that my blood had started flowing again. The birds were singing as if all creation was a choir of joy.

He spoke again, "You don't need to cling to me, Mary. I haven't gone to the Father yet." I was so afraid to lose him again, afraid that being with him was the only thing that would preserve this reality. Then quietly, patiently, and with a hint of laughter, he said, "Mary. You need to go and tell the others." I pulled back to ask, my voice breaking for fear, "But what about you, where are you going?" Tender and kind, he answered, "I am not going to the Father yet. But now everything is different, and you are to tell them I will go to my Father and your Father, to my God and your God."

It was one of those sayings of his, like so many others, that I would take away and ponder, repeat and savor: "My Father and your Father, My God and your God." And I knew it was pregnant with meaning that I could hardly grasp, meaning that was so glorious that all the heavens must be singing. He touched my face and laughed, and his laughter drew me back to the present. "Mary, you must go and tell the others. They don't understand yet." "Neither do I!" I exclaimed and laughed, too, even as the tears still trickled down my face. "You understand enough," he said, "and you need to go and tell them." At last I dared to believe it was not a dream, and he really would not disappear if I let him go. The birds would keep singing, and the sun would rise higher in the sky. I could hear the noise of a city coming back to life, and the people didn't know that the world had truly been remade. From this instant all of life was changed. Again he assured me, "It's all right, you'll see me again." And I turned and ran. I remember it felt almost like dancing and it must have puzzled some shopkeepers that I suddenly burst into laughter as I passed them setting up their stalls.

When I got back, the others were awake and sharing some food. I burst in, crying, "I've seen him, he was there—at the tomb." The conversations ceased. I saw the look of concern on Mary's face. Peter demanded, "What are you talking about now, Mary?" "He's alive! I saw him, and he told me to tell you." I was almost shouting, and I could see they didn't believe me. "Tell them, John," I insisted. "You know, don't you!" John spoke more slowly, "I didn't see him. But, yes." He paused. "Yes, I believe he's alive. I think that is what he was trying to tell us." I looked around the room. Some of them looked confused, anxious, concerned that maybe I was hysterical. Mary made me sit down, "Now start from the beginning," she said, "and tell us everything."

She asked someone to bring me a drink, and I told them every detail I could remember, from the roughness of his cloak against my cheek, to the birds singing the praises of a new earth, and every exact word he spoke. Some of them were still skeptical, especially the men. Maybe Susanna summed it up best. "We want to believe you Mary, oh, we so want to believe you. But I'm scared, it seems too good to be true." There was a murmur of agreement. Then Mary said to me, "I want to come back with you. Have something to eat, and we'll go back." That helped ground me again, and after a while a whole group of us returned. There was the empty tomb, with the linen cloths lying where the men had laid his body. I spoke to God in the hushed silence, "Our Father and our God, my Father and my God, show us your truth, and show us how to live in this new world." We sang the song that Mary had taught us, "My soul magnifies the Lord, and my spirit rejoices in my Savior."

That night Jesus came to us. This time there were a lot of us gathered together—with the doors locked, I may add, because they were afraid of the authorities. And suddenly there he was standing amongst us. Still, I could see by the looks on their faces that some of them were frightened, and some, like Susanna, hardly dared to believe. It was okay for me, because I knew as deeply as I knew anything that his risen life was real. It was hardest for the ones that weren't with us that night.

14

Doubting?—or Hiding

Thomas[1]

THOMAS WASN'T THERE THAT first night that Jesus came to us after the resurrection. He had run away like the others, but he hadn't come back. Thomas and I hadn't always related well. He had a brittle shell, and he often spoke reactively. It didn't surprise me when he turned up later in the week, looking awful and struggling terribly with the possibility that Jesus was alive. It was as though he didn't want to believe it. Yet without Jesus, life was hollow and totally meaningless. I understood a little of that and felt some sympathy for him. I asked him later to tell me about Jesus' resurrection from his perspective. The resurrection became the very core of our new life.

Thomas's Story

Doubting Thomas, they called me, if they did not know me, if they hadn't seen beneath the surface. Even as a little boy, I always had a soft heart.

1. John 11:16, 14:5, 20:24–29.

"He'll have to toughen up, that one," my father would say with a glance at my brothers. I was just as much a boy as they, climbing and running, scrapping and fighting. But that didn't stop the tears when I found a broken-winged butterfly or a fledgling fallen from its nest, too young to survive.

I felt for others, and my tears came quickly and unbidden. And when we sat at night and listened to the old ones tell the stories of our ancestors—of David's heart, broken over Absalom, of Jeremiah's tears over wayward Israel—why, my tears would come then, too. It seemed to me that this God of ours was a God of tears who wept for a people who went astray time after time.

I loved easily, too, and found heroes to adore. I had my heart broken more than once by girls whose eyes promised so much tenderness but turned elsewhere, or by the older boys I worshipped and tried to emulate. I did toughen up, I suppose, though maybe not in the way my father meant. I still felt deeply, but I learned to show it less readily, to guard my heart more carefully, to jump less quickly.

When they first told me of a Messiah, I remember my heart literally jumped in my chest and quickened its pace. My breath was almost knocked from me, but I held myself back. I asked how they could know and I acted hesitant to believe. I was not going to get taken in again. I watched and waited from the sidelines while others declared themselves more quickly than I. I saw his actions, but held my tongue. Hanging around the fringes, I listened to the talk.

I was sitting and watching at the lakeside one day, near others who were sorting fish and mending nets, when Jesus came, as if by chance, to crouch beside me. "What do you think, Thomas? What do you think the kingdom of God might be like if we really lived it?" He looked at me directly and kindly, and then looked away at the breeze ruffling the surface of the waves and the men shouting and bantering as they worked.

There was silence between us before he looked back and asked me, "What are you looking for, Thomas?" I wept then. For it seemed I knew already I could not have what I most longed for—a kingdom where the lion lay down with the lamb, the rich shared with the poor, and the men used their power to protect women and children and maimed. I found some stumbling words to tell him; I told him, too, how foolish it seemed to think these things possible. We sat in silence until he said, "Isn't it what our God calls us to seek?" As I slowly nodded, he added quietly, "It's what I'm giving *my* life for. What about you?" I gave my heart to him that day, totally and unreservedly. I dared to believe in the kingdom he talked about and to follow him anywhere, even to death if that's what he wanted. Not that I thought, in those early days, it would come to that.

In those heady, wondrous, early days, it seemed as though the kingdom really could come on earth. The blind *were* healed, and the lame walked. And better still, we lived as a band of brothers and sisters, sharing all we had in common. Sometimes the rich really did give what they had for the poor, and those with power understood Jesus enough to care for the powerless. Even when things began to go wrong, still I hoped. I saw some Pharisees catch the fire of his light, let go of their rigid rules, and soften to the deeper principles beneath. I believed what he said: that little seeds become spreading trees, that our God works in the margins, that the humble and the lowly will be transformed. This is the way the universe works. There is seedtime and harvest. Self-giving love reaps a hundredfold. His kingdom will come as we give ourselves in trust.

So when he was bent on going to that seat of power, Jerusalem, I was willing to walk with him into the mouth of death, the den of lions.

Only it was not as I expected. Death really was death. It was bloody and cruel and unbelieving. No quarter was given. He performed no final miracle, spoke no moving words to open their eyes and change their hearts. No legion of angels appeared. It was just whips and chains and meaningless cruelty.

I ran away. I could not stay with the women, bereft and courageous and weeping, with him every step of the way. My heart felt torn to shreds inside me. I ran away and hid where I could not hear the gossip. It felt like clashing swords inside my head, and I could not bear to be near any of it. I left the city and hid in the country-side in caves we knew. I wept and slept and woke to nothingness and slept again.

It was only after days had passed that I went back. I didn't know what else to do. Life had lost its shape and I didn't know where to begin to live again. I decided to see if I could find any of the others. Perhaps we could think about returning to Galilee and picking up our lives again, whatever that might mean.

What I found was totally outside my expectation. They were there, all of them: excited, joyful, expectant. "We have seen the Lord," they told me. The words did not even make sense. I remember the numbness when I first heard their news. My brain did not know the language they spoke. My broken heart had told my inner being never to believe again, never to listen to words of hope.

"I will not believe," I said. "Not unless I put my fingers in the holes of his wounds, and my hand in the sword thrust of his side." So I put up my shield to guard against any treacherous hope that would tear my heart again. But still I hung around them. It reminded me of the early days when I hung around but did not enter in. And in their kindness they cared for me. "You'll see Thomas. We couldn't believe it either. We don't even know what to do except to wait. Wait and see."

You know the story. You know how he came again to us. He came to me and looked me in the eye. He held out his scarred hand and said, with such deep kindness, with the deep kindness of this God who knows our changeful hearts, "Put your finger in my wounds, Thomas."

All I could do was fall at his feet and worship. He lifted me and held me as I sobbed out my pain and fear and confusion. "Ah, Thomas. Our God *is* God. Life does triumph over death, and mercy over judgment."[2]

2. Legend has it that Thomas took the gospel to India, that land of great disparity between the powerful and the powerless, the very rich and very poor, the whole and the maimed. Churches in India bear his name to this day, mute testimony to his faith in the kingdom which outlasts millennia.

Mary's Reflection

Thomas became one of the most solid of the men. His wavering faith settled into a pattern of utter devotion to a God who knew his heart and loved him into homecoming.

So there is my story. My story: a gathering of stories, a "midwifing" of transformed lives and journeys of new life.

I remember the words of Elisabeth, old faithful Elisabeth. She said that I would weave a tapestry of darkness and light, that others may see the picture and know the faithfulness of a God who stoops to us. He stoops in his birth as a naked baby in a place of poverty and in his dying as a tortured man, nailed to a crossbar of wood. But in between, shows us a way to live that makes joy possible, joy in the midst of suffering and joy in the face of death.

I offer these stories to you, brothers and sisters. Pilgrims in a broken world, may you know that death could not hold him, nor will death hold us. In his rising to new life, so do we rise, to live in service to one another and to the world that our God created as good and continues to recreate in deep goodness.

Amen. Come, Lord Jesus.

Printed in Australia
AUOC02n0852030414
260521AU00005B/7/P

9 781625 645449